Politics and
Religious
Authority

**Recent Titles in
Contributions to the Study of Religion**

POLITICS AND RELIGIOUS AUTHORITY

*American Catholics Since the
Second Vatican Council*

RICHARD J. GELM

Contributions to the Study of Religion,
Number 36

GREENWOOD PRESS
Westport, Connecticut • London

Library of Congress Cataloging-in-Publication Data

Gelm, Richard J.
    Politics and religious authority : American Catholics since the
Second Vatican Council / Richard J. Gelm.
       p. cm.—(Contributions to the study of religion, ISSN
0196–7053 ; no. 36)
    Includes bibliographical references and index.
    ISBN 0–313–28903–4 (alk. paper)
    1. Christianity and politics—Catholic Church—History—20th
century. 2. Catholic Church—United States—History—1965–
3. Catholics—United States—Attitudes. 4. Vatican Council (2nd :
1962-1965) 5. Catholic Church—United States—Teaching office—
History of doctrines—20th century. 6. Church—Authority—History
of doctrines—20th century. 7. Catholic Church—United States—
Bishops—History—20th century. 8. United States—Church
history—20th century. I. Title. II. Series.
BX1407.P63G45   1994
282′.73′09045—dc20   93-1650

British Library Cataloguing in Publication Data is available.

Library of Congress Catalog Card Number: 93–1650
ISBN: 0–313–28903–4
ISSN: 0196–7053

First published in 1994

Greenwood Press, 88 Post Road West, Westport, CT 06881
An imprint of Greenwood Publishing Group, Inc.

Printed in the United States of America

The paper used in this book complies with the
Permanent Paper Standard issued by the National
Information Standards Organization (Z39.48–1984).

10 9 8 7 6 5 4 3 2 1

To my mother and father
and John, Eileen, Diane, and Carolyn

Contents

Tables

Preface

The present study seeks to investigate the political effects of the Second
Vatican Council. Over the past three decades since the Council, the Roman
Catholic Church has been in a transitional phase, grappling with attempts
to find a balance between the forces of continuity and change. This struggle
has compelled the Church to reassess its role in politics and has left many
wondering what influence the Church still possesses.

Chapter 1 introduces the central theme that religion and politics are
connected in complex and enduring ways. The religious influence on
politics can be seen on multiple levels. As change occurs in one realm its
impact is often felt in the other.

Chapter 2 addresses religious contributions to political development.
Strong arguments can be made that religion was making significant contributions to the political development of the Western world long before the
rise of liberal democracy. The Catholic Church, more so than any other single
institution during the Middle Ages, served as a unifying force in society,
giving legitimacy to political institutions and processes. Although the
Church sought initially to impede democratic changes, eventually it became
a contributing force for political democracy in the West. As its more direct
connection with the government was severed, the Church sought to maintain
its influence by serving as a moral critic of society, helping to affect the
political values that serve as a basis for political culture.

While the connection between religion and culture has historically been
strong, the religious influence here is also changing. This is the topic of

chapter 3. Church teaching and its transmission through the church community can affect the political attitudes and outlook of religious followers.
Religious values often serve as the underpinnings of cultural and political
values. But these values are continually challenged.

The hope of church fathers at the Second Vatican Council was for a
transformation of cultures. Their blueprint for change is the topic of
chapter 4. This watershed event in Catholic history reflected profound
changes in the social and political outlook of the Church and in its social
teaching and led to new approaches for developing and teaching that
message.

Among the most significant changes stemming from the Council has
been the increased political activism of America's Catholic bishops.
Chapter 5 traces this change within the American hierarchy. I use the
results from my survey of American bishops to uncover cleavages within
the hierarchy and to assess prospects for short- and long-term changes
within the American Church. The bishops' views on a variety of political,
social, and religious issues were solicited through a 95-item questionnaire
mailed to all of the nearly 380 American bishops. Responses were received
from 150 bishops during 1989–1990. In addition to their answers to
closed-ended questions, bishops were invited to elaborate on their views
by way of written comments. Nearly one-third of the respondents offered
explanatory remarks. These are also used in this study.

The effects of Vatican II and the bishops' teaching on lay Catholics are
the topics of chapter 6. With inspiration from the Council, American
Catholics have a new maturity and sense of independence, which may
make the authoritarian attempts by some clerics to suppress dissent within
the Church more difficult and divisive. American Catholics cannot be
expected to faithfully follow every pronouncement of the bishops. They
reserve for themselves the right to use their own conscience in these
matters. But this does not negate a connection between religion and the
politics of American Catholics. The rules of the game have changed since
Vatican II. The church can no longer rely on its claim to authority. It must
pursue new methods to remain relevant in a changing world.

I would like to thank the many people who helped make this study
possible. To the faculty in the Department of Political Science at the
University of California, Davis, especially Ed Costantini, Alex Groth, and
Larry Wade, I extend sincere thanks for their support and assistance. I
thank Martin Marty and Thomas Reese, who read my manuscript and
offered insightful commentary. Special appreciation goes to the Catholic
bishops who responded to my survey, particularly Bishop Francis Quinn
of the diocese of Sacramento, California, who gave me encouragement to

undertake the enterprise of surveying the American hierarchy. Zoila Garcia was a great help in preparing the final manuscript and I thank her. Most of all, however, I would like to thank my family. My father and mother, Richard Henry Gelm and June Catherine Gelm, are due the highest gratitude for nurturing my interest in religion and politics and providing steadfast support. But I alone am responsible for the arguments presented here and I take full blame for any and all errors.

Chapter 1 _____

Introduction

> No longer on the edge of society but in the middle; we now have our
> best chance to restore the idealism of the nation's heritage. Gospel
> values should challenge us to give dignity and infinite value to each
> human—lift an individualistic, consumer-ridden society to go beyond
> self-serving interest and be a model for all nations. Pastorals are only
> words unless put into action. New people—new cultures force us to
> realize for all the American dream.
> Comments of an American Catholic Bishop (1989)

Questions concerning the impact of religion on political and cultural
beliefs and action have been of interest to social scientists for many years,
but only recently have they become topics of serious study in the field of
political science. The emerging involvement of evangelical and fundamentalist Protestant clergy in presidential elections has attracted attention
to the important connection between religion and politics.[1] But one group
that has received less attention from scholars is American Catholics. In a
predominantly Protestant country, American Catholic politics has been
treated as a kind of residual component of American political culture. This
treatment is no longer warranted.

Roman Catholicism is now the largest religious denomination in the
United States. In recent years, the Catholic presence in American politics
has reached new highs. Once denied equal access, Catholics have moved
into all levels of economic and political power. American Catholics have
reached economic parity with their Protestant counterparts.[2] Roman

Catholics comprised the single largest bloc in the 102nd Congress, with 122 Catholic members of the House of Representatives and 20 Catholic senators.[3] Catholic religious leaders have also reached national prominence. American Catholic bishops have commanded widespread attention with their pastoral statements on politics and economics.

With the ascendance to the national agenda of politically sensitive issues such as civil rights, school prayer, and abortion, many members of the clergy have been actively seeking to influence political debate. This has been as true of American Catholic bishops as the leaders of any other denomination. Individual bishops have reprimanded politicians supporting segregation, legalized abortion, and the death penalty.[4] Through the National Conference of Catholic Bishops (NCCB), American prelates have taken positions on issues ranging from abortion to traffic safety.[5] With their highly publicized pastoral letters including "The Challenge of Peace" and "Economic Justice for All," Catholic bishops reached center stage as political-religious leaders.[6] As the influence of mainline Protestant leaders declines, some look to the Catholic bishops to fill the moral leadership vacuum. The rising influence of Catholic bishops in the United States has prompted some to speak of a "Catholic moment" in America.[7]

The growing public status of Catholic bishops and their increased willingness to engage in the political dialogue stem not only from the improved social status of American Catholics in general, but from deeply felt beliefs about the role of the Catholic Church in the world. The bishops increasingly see themselves in the role of national moral teachers. This mission is given sustenance by reforms in the Church over the last three decades. The Catholic political experience since the 1960s cannot be viewed outside of the context and influence of the Second Vatican Council. While the Church has taught throughout its history that social and political questions cannot be separated from moral principles, Vatican II was a catalyst for bishops to find new ways to implement that teaching. A search for ways to link religious morality and politics drives American bishops in their political activism.

THE RELIGION AND POLITICS CONNECTION

Max Weber's controversial thesis on the connection between Protestant theology and the development of capitalism serves as the premier example of social scientific attempts to find linkage between religious belief and societal development.[8] The power of ideas, whether they have their origin in religion, politics, science, or literature, cannot be self-contained. Unfortunately, since the nineteenth century, the pursuit of knowledge in institutions of higher learning has been restricted by the tendency to compartmentalize disciplines. This downplays the interconnections between fields. Industrialists promoted the benefits derived from the assembly line method and colleges and universities borrowed the principle.[9] The American system of higher education emphasizes the autonomy of distinct disciplines and professions. A more complete understanding of political phenomena, however, requires a recognition of the contributions of history, economics, psychology, sociology, and religion.

This study investigates the religious roots of politics on several levels. The religious influence permeates the fabric of society. Because of the powerful nature of religious phenomena, religion cannot be separated from other aspects of the human experience. While defining religion is itself problematic, given the varieties of religious experience, the definition offered by Clifford Geertz is useful in that it conveys the far-reaching influence of religion that is common to all denominations. According to Geertz, "Religion is a system of symbols which acts to establish powerful, persuasive, and long-lasting moods and motivations in men by formulating conceptions of a general order of existence and clothing these conceptions with such an aura of factuality that the moods and motivations seem uniquely realistic."[10] These "moods and motivations" are likely to influence an individual in many facets of his life experience, including the political.

While attempts by religious leaders to influence political decisions illustrate a more obvious interaction between the realms of religion and politics, the connection goes much deeper. On the less obvious but more enduring effects of religion, William Miller points out that

there is also a still more important, if less measurable, *indirect* and long-term effect of the religious tradition upon the nation's politics. This is the impact of ways of thinking, believing, and acting in religious matters upon the shape of the mind, which impact affects the way other fields, like politics, are understood. Such effects, seeping down into the national character, may be discernible not only in clergymen and church people but in members of the society at large.[11]

Since Gerhard Lenski's pioneering work on religion and society, social scientists have sought to clarify empirically the connection between religion and politics.[12] The renaissance occurring in the study of religion and politics, spawned by the political activism of Protestant ministers in recent electoral politics, has followed in this tradition.[13] But the impact of religion endures well beyond any set of elections. We need to delve further than an analysis of elections or pronouncements by individual religious leaders to comprehend the depth of the religion and politics connection.

Too often religion is treated as a secondary or residual variable influencing political behavior. Class and economic variables are given high priority in explaining differences in political attitudes. The treatment of religion and politics often focuses on the political "result" of religious action.[14] This emphasis ignores the role of religion in shaping cultural attitudes about politics and in providing a legitimacy for authority. An important question to ask is the extent to which political ground rules and attitudes and beliefs about legitimate political action and authority are shaped by religious theology and belief. In other words, how does religion affect and interact with a nation's political culture?

The influence of religion on politics and culture can be seen on several different levels. By aligning with government during the Middle Ages and providing a stable and unifying force in society, the Church contributed to the development of powerful political institutions. With the rise of the secular state, the Church could no longer play such a direct role in society. But it would adapt and change. With the rise of liberal democracies in the West, the Church worked to mobilize voters and prepare them for participation in democratic government. It continues to search for ways to influence cultural beliefs that nourish political attitudes. American bishops as well as Protestant leaders seek to provide a moral basis for civic attitudes.

The processes by which religion affects political cultures can take a variety of forms. David Laitin identifies three sources of influence that can affect "political life."[15] At one level, the "pure doctrine" as articulated by theologians often speaks directly to questions of political morality. But this may be at a very high level of abstraction for the average individual to discern and make practical application to his political life. Rarely is anyone outside of the theologically educated circle aware of these specific teachings. They become relevant as they permeate through the cultural system of ideas. This second level of influence consists of a "practical religion" that is the result of "the interaction of doctrine and social origins of the ideas."[16] In other words, biblical or official church teachings may be interpreted quite differently depending upon the social context in which the religious doctrine is applied. For example, whether one views Jesus as an authoritarian lawgiver as opposed to a loving and forgiving brother of men may in part depend upon the extent to which authoritarian or egalitarian cultural values dominate a given society. Finally, the way in which this practical religion is shaped by believers ("the converted") to apply to their own lives contributes to a new "practical religion of the converted."[17]

Each individual must discern religion's relevance to his or her own life. How one orients toward religion, however, is often related to an orientation toward politics.

Many observers have attributed the political differences between religious groups to the varieties of theologies that differentiate religious traditions. While some contend that the political dissimilarities between members of separate religious groups are simply the result of varying social characteristics, including differences in income, education, ethnicity, and class, studies conducted where these variables are controlled still show political differences by religious denomination to be significant.[18] There is more that distinguishes Catholics from Protestants and Jews than can be accounted for by social characteristics.

The way in which one is oriented in his or her religious beliefs is related to how that person views the political world. Conservative or liberal religious orientations often correspond to similar political attitudes. In a seminal study of the religion and politics of members of the United States Congress, Peter Benson and Dorothy Williams found that "knowing how members scored on three or four of the religious themes can tell us as much or more about how they will vote than knowing whether they are Republican or Democrat."[19]

Neither politics nor religion, however, remain static. What happens when a religion undergoes changes, so that the theology is modified? Might political change also follow? The filtration of religious ideas through social institutions and through time presents a complex and dynamic system. While Protestants emphasize a more direct connection between biblical teaching and an individual's response, Roman Catholicism has long stressed the need for an institutional church to clarify religious doctrine and instruct the laity on questions of religious morality. When Catholic bishops issue pastoral letters on political and economic issues, they see their role as teachers, clarifying church doctrine so as to demonstrate how religion ought to guide the political values of their followers. But even within Catholicism the degree of emphasis on authority changes. The bishops admit that their statements do not carry the same authority as other statements of church doctrine.

But while the bishops have become national religious spokespersons, some wonder if anyone is listening. The extent to which the bishops' statements influence lay Catholics has been a point of much contention. One would be hard-pressed to argue that many Catholics have read the bishops' pastoral letters, or even have a real understanding of specific church teaching on politics and society. The request of 1928 Democratic nominee Al Smith, "Will somebody please tell me what in hell an encyclical is?" is indicative of the ignorance many Catholics have about formal church teaching.[20] Few Catholics are knowledgeable about the bishops' pastoral letters. Welch and colleagues found that even at the parish level, few had heard mention of these topics.[21] But while Catholics may not be aware of specific episcopal statements, they have been influenced by a broader religiocultural event that has transformed Catholicism and the Church's approach to the political world. They have been affected by Vatican II.

VATICAN II: A CATALYST FOR CHANGE

The increased political involvement of United States Catholic bishops must be placed in the context of major changes within Catholicism since the Second Vatican Council. This historic event saw the world's Roman Catholic bishops and cardinals assemble in Rome to reconsider the place of religion in the modern world. For three years, from 1962 to 1965, church fathers worked on documents to update church teaching and find new ways to maintain the Church's relevance in the world. The Council encouraged the world's bishops to more actively participate in social and political debate. And it inspired a greater sense of confidence and independence among lay Catholics, as it extended greater opportunities for the laity to participate in the decisions of the Church.

The impact of Vatican II reforms will be felt for decades, if not centuries, to come. The Council represents a fundamental shift by the Catholic Church with regard to its place in a changing world. Thomas O'Hara is correct when he notes that "for the most part social scientists have failed to appreciate the far-reaching effects the Second Vatican Council has had on the Catholic Church. Social scientists miss the political significance of an essential theme of Vatican II. That is, the church needs to be seen not just as a hierarchical and institutional entity; the church is comprised of all people, clerical and lay, united as 'The People of God.' "[22]

At the Second Vatican Council the Church came to accept the value in democracy, religious freedom, and the principle of separation of church and state. Not only did Vatican II help to foster a more liberal church outlook, but its emphasis on the collegial authority of bishops also helped to transform the American Catholic hierarchy, giving American prelates a greater sense of power within the Church.

If religious theology, or the Church's social teaching, is to have an impact in helping to shape individual political and social attitudes, it must in some way be disseminated to the public. The bishops see this as their responsibility. Once low-profile leaders of a minority religion, American bishops have become outspoken critics of American society as they have sought to reconcile the American system with what they view as the Gospel message.

The bishops' political and social teaching is not itself radically new. It stems from a long tradition. The Second Vatican Council teaching, to which the bishops aspire, is in a tradition of Catholic social teaching going back to Pope Leo XIII's encyclical *Rerum novarum*. Since that time the Church has consistently expressed a need for government regulation of the economy to protect the integrity of workers. Pope John Paul II's recent encyclical *Centesimuss annus*, commemorating the centenary of Leo's encyclical, follows in that tradition.

What has changed, however, is the vigor with which that teaching would be pushed. The Council encouraged bishops throughout the world to use episcopal conferences to bring the Church's social teaching to the peoples of all cultures. New tactics and strategies were developed. The authoritarian tactics used by the Church in the past had become outdated by the middle of the twentieth century. The importance placed on dialogue with the laity and people of other faiths departs sharply from the authoritarianism which had become synonymous with Catholicism.

To the extent that disagreement exists within the hierarchy itself, however, the absence of unanimity may help to further convey to Catholics that they are free to dissent. What the Second Vatican Council set in motion by encouraging dialogue and open inquiry is reflective of the changing role of religion in public life. Even when polls indicate that lay Catholics may disagree with their bishops on public policy issues, this does not necessarily indicate a lack of religious influence. Many religiously active Catholics respectfully dissent from the bishops, but they often do so with an informed conscience. Even if many Catholics lack a firm grasp of the bishops' teachings or the Second Vatican Council, the spirit or ideas of the Council have taken on a life of their own, permeating American Catholic culture, a culture already steeped in a tradition of independence and freedom.

Culture does not remain static, and neither does religion. American Catholics are no longer an immigrant minority, reluctant to speak critically of their society as they were earlier in American history. No longer is the Catholic Church the authoritarian protector that it sought to be during the Middle Ages and through the years of Protestant attacks. The rules of the game have changed. As Jay Dolan describes changes since the Council, "With the emergence of a new Catholicism, the immigrant Catholic ethos has changed. A new model of church and authority is replacing the old, monarchical, clerical concept of church and authority."[23] Vatican II is important in that it marks a shift in the tactics and message of church leaders and the laity. And American Catholic politics has not escaped its influence.

NOTES

1. See, for example, James L. Guth, Ted G. Jelen, Lyman A. Kellstedt, Corwin E. Smidt, and Kenneth D. Wald, "The Politics of Religion in America: Issues for Investigation," *American Politics Quarterly* 16, no. 3 (July 1988), esp. pp. 374–377; Charles W. Dunn, ed., *Religion in American Politics* (Washington, D.C.: Congressional Quarterly, 1989); James A. Reichley, *Religion in American Public Life* (Washington, D.C.: Brookings, 1985); Kenneth D. Wald, *Religion and Politics in the United States* (New York: St. Martin's Press, 1987); Kathleen Murphy Beatty and Oliver Walter, "A Group Theory of Religion and Politics: The Clergy as Group Leaders," *Western Political Quarterly*. 42, no. 1 (March 1989), pp. 129–146, and "Fundamentalists, Evangelicals and Politics," *American Politics Quarterly* 16, no. 1 (January 1988), pp. 43–59; James L. Guth, "Pastoral Politics in the 1988 Election: Protestant Clergy and Political Mobilization" (Paper presented at the 1989 Annual Meeting of the American Political Science Association, Atlanta, Georgia); Robert Lerner, Stanley Rothman, and S. Robert Lichter, "Christian Religious Elites," *Public Opinion* (March/April 1989), pp. 54–59. For earlier studies, see Jeffrey K. Hadden, *The Gathering Storm in the Churches* (Garden City, N.Y.: Doubleday, 1969); Harold E. Quinley, *The Prophetic Clergy: Social Activism among Protestant Ministers* (New York: Wiley, 1974).

2. See Andrew M. Greeley, *The American Catholic: A Social Portrait* (New York: Basic Books, 1977), p. 20.

3. Reported in Norman J. Ornstein, Thomas E. Mann, and Michael J. Malbin, *Vital Statistics on Congress: 1991–1992* (Washington, D.C.: Congressional Quarterly, 1992), pp. 35–37.

4. "Bishops Warn Politicians on Abortion," *New York Times*, November. 8, 1989, p. A10; "Legislator Barred from Catholic Rite," *New York Times*, November 17, 1989, p. A11; "New Brooklyn Bishop Named; To Bar Cuomo Over Abortion," *New York Times*, February 20, 1990, p. 1; Joe Feuerherd, "Death Penalty Makes Political Hay: Bishop Puts Lawmaker on New York Hot Seat," *National Catholic Reporter*, June 1, 1990, p. 3. For details on Bishop Hallinan's actions against segregationist politicians, see Thomas J. Shelley, "Paul J. Hallinan," in Gerald P. Fogarty, ed., *Patterns of Episcopal Leadership* (New York: Macmillan, 1989), pp. 235–249.

5. Stating that in "too many situations where death or injury occurs in automobile accidents, the driver is at fault," the bishops condemned reckless driving as "sinful." See "A Statement on Traffic Safety," November 17, 1957, in Hugh J. Nolan, ed., *Pastoral Letters of the United States Catholic Bishops*, vol.

2, 1941–1961 (Washington, D.C.: United States Catholic Conference, 1984), p. 200.

6. National Conference of Catholic Bishops, "The Challenge of Peace: God's Promise and Our Response" (Washington, D.C.: United States Catholic Conference, 1983); "Economic Justice for All: Catholic Social Teaching and The U.S. Economy" (Washington, D.C.: United States Catholic Conference, 1986).

7. Former Lutheran scholar and recent Catholic convert Richard J. Neuhaus argues that given the declining influence of mainline Protestant leaders, "this can and should be the moment in which the Roman Catholic Church in the United States assumes its rightful role in the culture-forming task of constructing a religiously informed public philosophy for the American experiment in ordered liberty" (Richard John Neuhaus, *The Catholic Moment* [San Francisco: Harper and Row, 1987], p. 283).

8. Max Weber, *The Protestant Ethic and the Spirit of Capitalism* (New York: Scribner's, 1958).

9. See Burton J. Bledstein, *The Culture of Professionalism: The Middle Class and the Development of Higher Education in America* (New York: Norton, 1976).

10. Clifford Geertz, "Religion as a Cultural System," in Donald R. Cutler, ed., *The Religious Situation* (Boston: Beacon Press, 1968), p. 668.

11. William Lee Miller, "American Religion and American Political Attitudes," in James Ward Smith and A. Leland Jamison, eds., *Religious Perspectives in American Culture* (Princeton: Princeton University Press, 1961), p. 83.

12. Gerhard Lenski, *The Religious Factor: A Sociological Study of Religion's Impact on Politics, Economics, and Family Life* (Garden City, N.Y.: Doubleday–Anchor, 1963).

13. See, for example, Steve Bruce, *The Rise and Fall of the New Christian Right: Conservative Protestant Politics in America 1978–1988* (Oxford: England: Clarendon Press, 1988).

14. See Daniel H. Levine, "Religion and Politics in Comparative and Historical Perspective," *Comparative Politics* 19, no. 1 (October 1986), pp. 95–122.

15. David D. Laitin, "Religion, Political Culture, and the Weberian Tradition," *World Politics* 30 (July 1978), pp. 563–592.

16. Ibid., p. 572.

17. Ibid.

18. See, for example, Kathleen Beatty and Oliver Walter, "Religious Preference and Practice: Reevaluating Their Impact on Political Tolerance," *Public Opinion Quarterly* 48, no. 1B (Spring 1984), pp. 318–329; Edward O. Laumann and David R. Segal, "Status Inconsistency and Ethnoreligious Group Membership as Determinants of Social Participation and Political Attitudes," *American Journal of Sociology* 77, no. 1 (July 1971), pp. 36–61; William S. Maddox, "Changing Electoral Coalitions from 1952–1976," *Social Science Quarterly* 60, no. 2 (September 1979), pp. 309–313; Frederick W. Grupp and William M. Newman, "Political Ideology and Religious Preference: The John Birch Society

and the Americans for Democratic Action," *Journal for the Scientific Study of Religion* 12, no. 4 (December 1973), pp. 401–413; Abraham Miller, "Ethnicity and Party Identification: Continuation of a Theoretical Dialogue," *Western Political Quarterly* 27 no. 3 (September 1974), pp. 479–490.

19. Peter L. Benson and Dorothy L. Williams, *Religion on Capitol Hill: Myths and Realities* (New York: Oxford University Press, 1986), p. 165.

20. Quoted in James Hennesey, "Roman Catholics and American Politics, 1900–1960: Altered Circumstances, Continuing Patterns," in Mark A. Noll, ed., *Religion and American Politics: From the Colonial Period to the 1980s* (New York: Oxford University Press, 1990), p. 313.

21. Michael Welch et al., "Pastoral Cues and Congregational Responses: Evidence from the 1989 NES Pilot Study" (Paper presented at the 1990 Annual Meeting of the American Political Science Association, San Francisco, California).

22. Thomas J. O'Hara, "The Catholic Lobby in Washington: Pluralism and Diversity among U.S. Catholics," in Mary C. Segers, ed., *Church Polity and American Politics: Issues in Contemporary American Catholicism* (New York: Garland, 1990), p. 145.

23. Jay P. Dolan, *The American Catholic Experience: A History from Colonial Times to the Present* (Garden City, N.Y.: Doubleday, 1985), p. 453.

Chapter 2 _____

Religion, Political Development, and Change

Guy Michelat and Michel Simon have noted that "most observers consider the tie between religion and politics a thing of the past."[1] Indeed, social scientists have long predicted a decline of religious influence in advanced, modern societies. Daniel Bell concludes that "from the end of the nineteenth century to the middle of the twentieth century, almost every sociological thinker . . . expected religion to disappear by the onset of the twenty-first century."[2] Yet religion endures. In the United States, overwhelming majorities express a belief in God, and many religious denominations are experiencing record growth. Religion remains a potent force in society. And politics has not escaped its influence.

America's attempt to separate church and state stems from a belief that religion and politics should not be mixed. Supreme Court decisions against government-sanctioned prayer in the schools and state aid to parochial schools illustrate attempts to erect what Thomas Jefferson called a "wall of separation" between religion and government.[3] Despite the theory and the predictions, however, the relationship between religion and politics is enduring and complex. While the close ties between churches and governments have been severed, church leaders demand a voice in the political decisions of society. They have assumed new roles and tactics in their attempt to continue to influence the political development of society. The sociological thinkers referred to by Daniel Bell accurately anticipated the threats to religion brought on by the forces of modernization. However, the presumption that religion's influence on politics would disappear proved inaccurate. Modernization and political development are separate (though related) phenomena.

POLITICAL DEVELOPMENT AND MODERNIZATION

The terms "political development" and "modernization" are often used interchangeably by political writers, and there are about as many definitions of these terms as there are authors. Bill and Hardgrave, however, stress the utility in differentiating between the two. While "development is most usefully understood in terms of a system's response capacity in relationship to demands," modernization refers "to those changes (not necessarily systematically related) associated with man's increasing control over his natural and social environments—changes associated most frequently with the technological and scientific revolution of the past four hundred years."[4] The advances in scientific technologies offer answers to questions that were previously left to religion, and they can offer opportunities for social advancement. But whether the political system can keep pace with the changes is a different question.

While modernization often leads to political development, the association is not always linear. Modernization can raise expectations and political demands, yet there is no certainty that the political system will adapt to meet them.[5] On the other hand, modernization is not necessarily a prerequisite for political development. In primitive societies where the political system satisfies the demands placed upon it, it could be argued that such a system is more fully developed than a more "advanced" society whose political development has not caught up with the demands brought on by the process of modernization.

Lucian Pye has summarized the themes common to the political development literature. "Political development," he contends, "is nation building." This requires: (1) a differentiation and specialization of political institutions, (2) a greater participatory role by the citizenry, and (3) a capacity for the system to adapt to and direct social and economic change.[6] Modernization, on the other hand, is a process that transcends the political. As Manfred Halpern points out, modernization "involves the transformation of all systems by which man organizes his society—the political, social, economic, intellectual, religious, and psychological systems."[7] Modernization and political development may occur simultaneously, but this is not guaranteed.. In fact, too rapid a change in the intellectual or religious realms might cause fear among political leaders who anticipate challenges from a new intelligentsia. Such fear may result in political crackdown and dictatorship. Modernizing forces within one realm may not keep pace with changes elsewhere.

The effects of modernization on religion and politics have been mixed. Modernization tends to coincide with political development and is often associated with a decline of religion. In premodern systems religion plays a more direct role in legitimizing and directing political change. Often it is the religious leaders who command the most respect within society and as a result possess the capacity to direct change. In modern systems political development is often associated with a move toward a more secular society and a break between the religious and the political. New elites within scientific and intellectual spheres often become those best able to direct highly technical change.

The fact that scientific advances associated with modernization offer rationalism to replace religious faith has usually led to the relegation of religion to an inferior position of importance and the recognition that religion no longer provides the only acceptable rationale for society. Political leaders come to rely more on new elites, and turn away from the guidance of religious leaders. The public's allegiance to church authority also dwindles.

The rise of an increasingly secular polity has been described by many theorists of political development. Almond and Powell, for example, tie political development to "the increased differentiation and specialization of political structures and the increased secularization of political culture."[8] According to Donald Smith, "The secularization of the polity has been the most fundamental structural and ideological change in the process of political development."[9]

Fred Riggs uses a light and prism analogy to illustrate the changing role of religion in the developing society. In traditional systems the religious and the political functions are "fused." The transmission of religious symbols and values are merged with the political and often provide the legitimacy for a ruling elite. As societies "develop," there is a greater separation of functions and the society becomes more "diffused." The religious and political become separate and distinct, like the rays of light passed through a prism.[10]

J. Milton Yinger makes a similar argument by use of a threefold descriptive typology of the evolution of societies and the changing role of religion. In stable primitive systems (and to a lesser extent in "mobile and complex" societies), religion and politics are reinforcing. Religious beliefs and practices work to socialize individuals to accept the political norms. In the next stage this "integrative relationship" is disrupted. Here, political leaders use religion in manipulative ways to maintain their position of authority, often through coercion. Religious doctrines are applied selectively as needed to justify the power of rulers. The final stage is marked by a break between the political and the religious, with each consigned to a separate sphere of influence.[11] Religious leaders tend their flocks, but avoid involvement in politics.

This break between the religious and the political is generally not a simple process. As new political elites seek to justify their legitimacy separate from the older religious leaders, a contest for the loyalty of the people is likely to ensue. The traditional religious elite often seeks to hold on to its authority. In response to their declining influence in society, churches often criticize the effects of modernization and the secularization of society. In this stage they may attempt to block the advance of scientific and political development. While in America the separation of church and state proceeded relatively smoothly, the French and Russian revolutions illustrate how tumultuous the break can be.

FUSION OF CHURCH AND STATE

Especially after the alliance with Constantine and the Roman Empire in the fourth century, Roman Catholicism provided a religious foundation upon which to organize society. The fusion of church and state signified the potential power of religion in legitimizing political systems. While the symbiotic relationship offered benefits to both sides, the formerly pagan Roman political rulers used Christian religious sanction to give legitimacy to their rule.[12] With the subsequent fall of the Roman Empire, the Church remained as the only source of centralized authority in society. "The papal movement," Renna argues, "was the single most dynamic source of inspiration to constructive action. This civilizing process worked towards the creation of new forms of cooperative efforts and material progress. The holy see provided a skeleton around which the body of 'Europe' could grow."[13] The building of the great cathedrals of Europe and the organization of communities around these projects are indicative of the Church's influence during the Middle Ages.

Bryan Wilson describes the central role of the Church this way:

Even before the nascent national states took shape, the Roman Church had acquired the function of legitimizing kings in their office, of superintending public affairs, of pronouncing on the legitimacy of wars, legal actions, and a variety of other public concerns, including the morality of economic activities. Christianity thus came to exercise powerful influence over constitutional, political, judicial, educational, and even economic issues . . . [T]he Church, more than any agency, provided the inspiration for European high culture. . . . The Church controlled learning in the universities; it promoted a lingua franca for educational discourse, and had for long a near-monopoly of its use.[14]

The Church's corporatist view of the proper social order served as a basis for the structuring of society. This view stressed the primacy of church authority and the interconnection of all people in a hierarchical system. While clear distinctions were made between individuals' proper places in society, all were recognized as part of a total community, each with his own role. The influence of this belief system did not end with the Middle Ages. By 1903, Pope Pius X still maintained that it was "in conformity with the order established by God that there should be in human society, princes and subjects, patrons and proletariat, rich and poor, learned and ignorant, nobles and plebeians."[15] Christians, he argued, "should maintain that distinction of classes which is proper to a well-constituted city, and should seek, for human society, the character that God, its author, has given it."[16] This view of a class-based society, while consistent with medieval political thought, was clearly outmoded by the twentieth century.

Forces working toward new political arrangements and a separation of church and state were developing long before the reign of Pius X. And the role of the Church in society had already begun to shift, so that the development of modern political institutions could also gain sustenance from Christianity.

Prior to the eleventh century the lines between church and state were blurred. But beginning in the eleventh century, the higher clergy in the Church began to view their role as that of social critic seeking to shape society according to biblical principles. To achieve the independence necessary to comment critically, it became necessary for the Church to break free from the grip of political leaders who used religion to justify their power. Pope Nicholas II (d. 1061) made two significant contributions to this effort by issuing the famous Electoral Decree, putting the power of papal election into the hands of the cardinals, and then securing military assistance from the Normans of Sicily to enforce the decree.[17] The Church, independent of the state, would choose its own leaders.

With this break and the development of the modern nation-states of Europe, however, church influence declined. Monarchs now possessed power bases independent of Rome. And with the Protestant Reformation, the Church lost religious influence as well. When the Catholic Church was challenged by the Protestants in the sixteenth century, an era of religious and political pluralism was ushered in.[18] While the order and stability preferred by the Church allowed Europe to survive the Middle Ages and provided a nurturing environment in which society eventually matured past the need for the Church's protective boundaries, it was not conducive to changes necessary for scientific and political development.

Democracy and science flourished in a growing atmosphere of inquiry, and the effects of this growth spread far past Europe. In America, religious pluralism offered the seeds of political pluralism. The multitude of religious sects there made an official state church untenable and forced public recognition of the need for tolerance. The First Amendment prohibition on the establishment of a state religion and protection of the free exercise of religion officially formalized the church and state separation.

For the Roman Catholic Church, however, the acceptance of its declining position came slowly. The Church did not formally accept the virtues of religious and political pluralism until the Second Vatican Council in the 1960s, and it fought long and hard to maintain its position.

CONTEST FOR AUTHORITY

The Roman Catholic Church has often fought to restrict forces seen as a threat to its authority. When science began to answer questions that only religion could answer before, religion lost its mystery and majesty. While a monopoly on "truth" provided religious leaders their ultimate source of power, the dissemination of knowledge and scientific challenges necessary for technological change was taken as an attack to be repelled. In response to the challenges from the scientific revolution and the Enlightenment, the Church lashed out against the forces of secularization and modernization. Pope Gregory XVI (d. 1846) and Pope Pius IX (d. 1878) openly opposed the modernizing tendencies in society. Their position is articulated clearly in Pius IX's "Syllabus of Errors" (1864). In this document Pius proclaimed that the pope "cannot and should not be reconciled and come to terms with progress, liberalism, and modern civilization."[19] The subsequent Vatican I dogmatic definition of papal primacy and papal infallibility was an attempt by the Church to reassert its moral teaching authority in the face of secular (and religious) attacks.

American bishops echoed Rome's warnings against the "dangers of rationalism" in an 1884 pastoral letter. "Could we rely fully on the innate good sense of the American people . . . ," they argued, "there might seem comparatively little danger of the general diffusion of those wild theories. . . . But when we take into account the daily signs of growing unbelief, and see how its heralds not only seek to mould the youthful mind in our colleges and seats of learning, but are also actively working against the masses, we cannot but shudder at the dangers that threaten us in the future."[20]

The Church had reasons for fearing scientific and intellectual challenges, only two of which were loss of credibility and loss of morality. It was fighting to maintain its position as sole declarer of truth, but the goal was not power for power's sake. The flock was beginning to stray, and strict control was viewed as a necessary price to pay to secure the salvation of souls. The Church's apprehension about the advances of scientific knowledge was, in part, linked to a common belief that the attainment of knowledge is often associated with a decay of the soul. "Whether for Greek or Christian, the conception of moral and spiritual decline is inextricably tied up with man's possession of faculties which are crucial to his material and cultural progress on earth."[21] The anti-intellectual strain of Catholicism derived from a view that equated science with atheism.[22] The Church's "censorship mentality" was fostered by such fears.[23] Positive change, however, often requires that existing authority and "truth" be challenged.

This rigidity of doctrine contrasted sharply with the progressive tenets of the Reformation, the Enlightenment and the scientific revolution. The new Protestant theology was more conducive to the development of new nation-states in Europe. Protestant theology gave a legitimacy to political changes taking place in Europe at that time, illustrating the capacity for change within religion as well. The Catholic Church sought through a Counter-Reformation to clean up the internal corruption that had left it vulnerable to attack. But it continued to demand an outdated authoritarianism. In a rapidly modernizing world, this rigid rule sought to stifle scientific advances and block the forces of democracy. Catholicism, once a leading force in the development of political systems, became an impediment.

PROTESTANTISM AND AMERICAN CATHOLICISM: RELIGION IN TRANSITION

It is difficult to determine the extent to which the rise of Protestantism was a response to, or a contributing force for, the radical political, social, philosophical, and economic changes taking place in sixteenth-century Europe.[24] But the new theologies of Protestantism offered a more dynamic view of the world than did medieval Catholicism and helped legitimize the processes of modernization and change. The Reformation itself was an attack upon the establishment, and in this sense it was radical. Protestantism offered justification for attacks on the existing power structure, at least until it was absorbed into the state structure. Peter Blickle maintains that the Reformation initially opened the door to social protest and the use of biblical justifications for social reform, but as Lutheranism came under state control, this radicalism was squelched. As Lutheranism became closely associated with the state, it also became a conservative force in society.[25]

Whereas the Roman Catholic Church had been a defender of the feudal system, and sought to slow the forces of liberalism, a redefinition of Christianity produced a source for defending the changes to bring that system down. The new Protestant theology offered a mentality more conducive to the advance of capitalism and democracy. The Calvinist conception of "calling" and an emphasis on self-sacrifice, hard work, and frugality presented a work ethic consistent with the needs of a capitalist economic order.[26] Martin Luther's proposition that "every man is his own priest" stressed an equality of men upon which democratic ideals could be built.

Though far from advocating democracy, John Calvin's philosophy offered ideas consistent with those calling for limited government. Arguing for a dispersion of power, Calvin noted that, "the vice or imperfection of men . . . renders it safer and more tolerable for the government to be in the hands of many, that they may afford each other mutual assistance and admonition, and that if any one arrogate to himself more than is right, the many may act as censors and masters to restrain his ambition."[27] Perhaps foreshadowing the new American system with its scheme for a divided Congress, Calvin conceded, "I shall by no means deny that either aristocracy or a mixture of aristocracy and democracy far excels all others."[28]

And within American Protestantism, Perry Miller maintains, "there was an irrepressibly democratic dynamic . . . though all good Protestants strove to stifle it."[29] With their belief in the basic sinfulness of man, Puritans harbored no false illusions about the potential for abuse of power. John Cotton argued, "It is necessary therefore, that all power that is on earth be limited, Church-power or other."[30] Richard Mather also explained the need to balance power: "We give the exercise of all Church power," he said, "neither all to the people excluding the Presbytery, nor all to the Presbytery excluding the People. For this were to make the government of the Church either meerly Democraticall [*sic*], or meerly Aristocraticall [*sic*], neither of which we believe it ought to be."[31] While stopping short of endorsing democracy, Puritans were making concessions to the idea of a more republican form of government.

Protestant clergymen took up the fight for political independence from the British monarchy. Alan Heimert argues that Protestant clergy were integrally responsible for stirring the colonists to revolution in a quest for a "virtuous" republic: "It was the Calvinist conception of the pastor's role and his relationship to his people that led to the creation of an institutional framework within which men responded enthusiastically, in the 1770's, to the verbal promptings of their spiritual guides."[32] Though Heimert's thesis has been questioned as to the degree to which ministers fueled this enthusiasm, it must be recognized that republican ideas were being disseminated from the pulpit.

Jonathan Mayhew's *Discourse Concerning Unlimited Submission* exemplifies the extent to which the clergy were preaching the ideals of the revolution. On the rule of King George III, he argued, "Nothing can well be imagined more directly contrary to common sense, than to suppose that millions of people should be subjected to the arbitrary, precarious pleasure of one single man . . . who has naturally no superiority over them in point of authority."[33] American Protestant leaders helped to bridge egalitarian principles with Christianity.

Less influential than prominent Protestants were Catholic clergy, who, due to attacks from a hostile Protestant majority, sought to maintain a low profile. But American Catholicism was moving away from the authoritarianism of the Church in Europe. American Catholics gave endorsement to a system of religious tolerance. The two Catholic delegates at the American Constitutional Convention heartily endorsed provisions to keep church and state separate. As John Tracy Ellis argues, "The final solution to the perplexing problem of religion as embodied in the Constitution and Bill of Rights was received by no American religious group with more genuine satisfaction than by the Catholics."[34] A persecuted Catholic minority had much to gain from legal protection and public tolerance.

Despite attempts by the Church in Europe to stem the tide of democracy and political and religious pluralism, American Catholics embraced the idea of religious freedom and political equality. The eminently astute French observer of nineteenth-century America, Alexis de Tocqueville, viewed American Catholicism as not inconsistent with the tenets of democracy:

I think that the Catholic religion has erroneously been regarded as the natural enemy of democracy. Among the various sects of Christianity, Catholicism seems to me, on the contrary, to be one of the most favorable to equality of condition among men. In the Catholic Church the religious community is composed of only two elements: the priest and the people. The priest alone rises above the rank of his flock, and all below him are equal. . . .If, then, the Catholic citizens of the United States are not forcibly led by the nature of their tenets to adopt democratic and republican principles, at least they are not necessarily opposed to them; and their social position, as well as their limited number, obliges them to adopt these opinions.[35]

Andrew Greeley and Henry Steele Commager attribute to American Catholicism a significant role in the political development of America. As Greeley argues, the ethnic differentiation that characterized American Catholicism "provided the immigrants and their children and grandchildren with considerable political, social, economic, and psychological advantages. The ethnic group became one of the avenues to political power for immigrants. It provided a special market in which the emerging business and professional class within the immigrant community could build its own economic base."[36] The power of religious communities to nurture social solidarity and affect social and political attitudes is illustrated by the American Catholic experience.

According to Henry Steele Commager, "It might, indeed, be maintained that the Catholic church was, during this period, one of the most effective of all agencies for democracy and Americanization. Representing as it did a vast cross section of the American people, it could ignore class, section, and race; peculiarly the church of the newcomers, of those who all too often were regarded as aliens, it could give them not only spiritual refuge but social security."[37]

Church leaders often lauded the American system. America's Catholic bishops became strong advocates of the government, frequently giving public endorsement to the American system of democracy. In 1884 American bishops praised the founders as having been inspired by God: "We consider the establishment of our country's independence, the shaping of its liberties and laws as a work of special Providence, its framers 'building wiser than they knew,' the Almighty's hand guiding them."[38]

Such praise and admiration for American democracy was not equaled in Rome, however, where Pope Leo XIII warned against "Americanism." In 1899 the pope issued the letter *Testem benevolentiae*, which included a condemnation of ideas the pope believed threatened the Old World. Americanism was equated with attempts to modernize the Church, to bring it in sync with modernizing change.[39]

Rome's trouble with American democracy was not simply that it believed hierarchical government to be inherently better, but that democracy was too closely aligned with the forces of liberalism. The liberal emphasis on individuality rather than community virtue was viewed in conflict with the Church's view of an "organic" society.[40] More immediate threats, however, may have been behind the attack on liberalism. To endorse the

ideas of separation of church and state, individual liberty, and press
freedom would put the Church on the side of those who would most like
to destroy it. Intense anti-Catholic sentiment in the United States and
France was not uncommon among those challenging authoritarian power
and pushing for democracy. And this point did not go unnoticed in the
American Church.

Division between liberals and conservatives within the American
Church also developed. In the early twentieth century, liberal and conservative forces within the American hierarchy argued over the issue of
Church authoritarianism. Liberals felt that the Church should accept the
virtues of tolerance and seek more cordial relations with Protestants. They
believed that it should recognize the inevitability of historical change and
reconcile itself with modern society. Conservatives, however, stood steadfast to the view that religious principles could not be "compromised" to
accommodate the changing world. They demanded strict obedience to
Church authority.[41]

In 1907, Pope Pius X sided with conservatives and forcefully warned
against the "errors" of the modernists.[42] Pius initiated a crackdown on
priests who espoused modernist ideas, requiring priests to take an oath
against such tendencies. Fear of Rome killed any intellectual spirit that
might have resided in seminaries and Catholic institutions of higher
learning.[43] American Catholicism entered a dark age as conservativism
and strict obedience to Rome overshadowed free intellectual inquiry. But
a new day would come. The Church would change.

The liberal American position would eventually win favor at the Second
Vatican Council. American clerics were prominent proponents of a declaration on religious liberty and a recognition of the value of political
pluralism.[44] The contribution of American bishops to the debate on
religious liberty may have been "their finest hour in the Council."[45] John
Courtney Murray, more so than perhaps any other Council participant,
articulately argued for the principles of American democracy. He forcefully sought to reconcile Catholicism with the American way of life,
extolling the virtues of religious pluralism and liberal democracy.[46]

THE CHURCH RESPONDS TO REALITIES OF
LIBERAL DEMOCRACY

Despite its rhetorical opposition to democracy, the Church was compelled to accept political realities. It learned how to work within a pluralist
system long before its formal acceptance came with the Second Vatican
Council. By the nineteenth century, churches in Europe and the United

States had lost the level of influence they once wielded and the realms of church and state were more clearly distinct.[47] To avoid being left behind, the Church had to reconcile itself to a new political order.

The development of the nation-states in Europe signified the failure of Pope Gregory's dream of a united Europe. A religious appeal (and papal alliances) proved inadequate to achieve such a monumental feat. The Church was now one among many competing interest groups in society, and it was forced to mobilize through new political instruments, political parties, and interest groups to affect the political process. In so doing, however, it helped to foster further political development by socializing its followers to become politically active citizens. In this way, as it sought to retain a moral influence on society, the Church would make new contributions to the development of modern political democracy.

By encouraging their followers to get involved politically, churches continue to make contributions in the facilitation of democracy. The mobilization of citizens into the political process is a necessary requisite for the development of the "civic culture."[48] Since organized religion provides a basis for political learning and recruitment, it has, in this century, served as a political mobilizer for people who would otherwise be nonparticipants. "Whereas in traditional societies, religion is a mass phenomenon, politics is not; in transitional societies, religion can serve as the means by which the masses become politicized."[49]

The Catholic Action program, set forth by Pope Pius XI in the 1930s, prepared the laity to take up political roles in European society. Many of the leaders of the Christian Democratic parties received training through the Catholic Action program.[50]

The Anti-Revolutionary party in the Netherlands and the Christian Democratic movement in many European countries also received a boost from the churches. The interconfessional Christian Democratic Union (CDU) party in Germany has been credited with pulling German society together after the fall of the Nazis.[51] The attempted union between the Protestants and Catholics under the CDU offered a centrist alternative to the other radical elements in Germany. Because of its wide appeal, the CDU had to be pragmatic, and neither the Protestants nor the Catholics were able to enforce dogmatic theology on the party. Frederic Spotts argues that "the [Catholic] church's fateful act . . . was the decision not to reestablish the Center party but instead to support an interconfessional party independent of the church. In giving up the institutional link between church and party, the bishops crossed a great practical and psychological divide. The ultimate, if unintentional, effect was to emancipate German Catholics politically."[52]

In Italy the Church actively sought to aid the Italian Christian Democratic Party. Indicating the extent of papal influence in Italian elections, Pius XII told voters before the 1946 Constituent Assembly elections that they had a choice between "the champions and the destroyers of Christian civilisation."[53] Though stated indirectly, it was clear that the "champions" of Christian civilization resided in the Christian Democratic Party. While the Church avoided making explicit endorsements in favor of a particular party, it was less reluctant to speak out against specific parties. The 1949 papal decree refusing the sacraments to supporters of the Communist party was intended to apply worldwide.[54]

Particularly since Vatican II, however, the Church has retreated from such overt attempts to influence voters. Rome has responded to the realities of pluralism and modernization by abandoning its attempt to provide an all-encompassing social doctrine. Catholic prelates shy away from specifically endorsing parties or candidates. Indicating the reluctance of church leaders to commit to one political ideology, Pope Paul VI acknowledged that "in view of the varied situations in the world, it is difficult to give one teaching to cover them all or to offer a solution which has universal value. This is not our intention or even our mission."[55]

In the American Church, leaders are very defensive against partisan connections. In response to critics who labeled their economic pastoral letter as propaganda for the Democratic party, Archbishop Rembert Weakland responded, "The letter is not a political instrument of either the Democratic or Republican Party. It is not the Church's role to come up with economic theories and solutions or take partisan positions, but the Church has to be concerned about how economic issues affect the lives of people. Not to do that would be to shirk what religion is all about."[56]

Weakland's explanation notwithstanding, several bishops have come very close to making outright partisan endorsements.[57] New York Cardinal John O'Connor's statements against the Democratic presidential ticket in 1984 dogged the Catholic vice presidential nominee Geraldine Ferraro throughout the campaign. Ferraro and other Catholic politicians who, though personally opposed to abortion, did not seek laws to outlaw the practice, were targeted by the hierarchy. San Diego Bishop Leo Maher was more forceful in his attempt to sanction a pro-choice Catholic politician. In 1989 Maher denied communion to California State Senate candidate Lucy Killea.[58] In other action New York Bishop Austin Vaughn suggested that Governor Mario Cuomo and other pro-choice Catholic politicians may risk going to hell for not using their position of influence to fight abortion.[59] And Cardinal O'Connor raised speculation that the excommunication of pro-choice Catholic politicians is possible.[60]

These actions, however, serve as exceptions to a general rule bishops hold not to make candidate endorsements or take public positions in partisan races. In our survey, only 5 percent of American bishops indicated that they have taken a public stand on a candidate for public office (see chapter 5). Most recognize the threat to their credibility should they be seen as telling people how to vote.[61]

NEW TACTICS

While the influence on politics of modern-day religious leaders no longer rivals that of medieval popes, the Church has adopted new tactics as well as a new message. For Catholicism, Vatican II is a watershed in history. The central message of the Council, which emphasized the Church as the "People of God," supported a greater role for the laity in the formulation and implementation of church policy.

Vatican II was an admission that the place of the Church in society had changed and that new approaches would be necessary to maintain the Church's relevance in the modern world. Hundreds of years earlier Pope Gelasius recognized the forces leading to a separation of church and state. He spoke of the Church and state on dual tracks, but argued that the Church retains a role as moral teacher. This role constitutes what American bishops see as their political mission. "Why do we address these matters fraught with such complexity, controversy and passion?" the bishops wrote in 1983. "We speak as pastors, not politicians. We are teachers, not technicians. We cannot avoid our responsibility to lift up the moral dimensions of the choices before our world and nation."[62]

While they demand the right to criticize the moral actions of government, nevertheless, their tactics have changed. Bishops can no longer rely upon strict obedience from their followers. Punitive sanctions no longer instill the fear to force compliance. Responding to Rome's concerns about Americans' deviation from official church teaching, St. Louis Archbishop John May told the Vatican that many American Catholics "consider the divine right of bishops as outmoded as the divine right of kings. . . . Authoritarianism," he stated, "is suspect in any area of learning or culture. . . . Individual freedom is prized supremely."[63]

Attempts to use religious sanction against pro-choice politicians have backfired on the bishops. These threats no longer carry the force they may have in the past. Few Catholic politicians seem willing to shift their position on abortion to accommodate the bishops.[64] Pennsylvania State Senator Vincent Fumo's position is typical: "My religion will not interfere with what I perceive to be my role in government. I did not take the oath as an ambassador for the Catholic Church."[65]

To the dismay of Republican strategists, the bishops' actions may tilt the advantage to pro-choice Democrats. As one senior Republican strategist complained, "This is the worst kind of thing for us. At a time when we are struggling with the painful contradictions of abortion in the party, all we need is the Catholic Church jumping in with both feet and frightening people to death on the church-state issue."[66]

A public backlash against the bishops' political activism may also be developing. Surveys indicate Catholics resent the bishops' intervention in electoral politics when it comes to the issue of abortion.[67] It appears that San Diego Bishop Leo Maher's communion ban against California State Senate candidate Lucy Killea may actually have given the pro-choice candidate a boost in support. In a solidly Republican district the underdog Democrat scored a big upset.

The bishops, however, feel pressure from Rome and the right wing of the Church. As Duluth Bishop Roger Schwietz put it, "There are many Catholics who think that the whole abortion issue rests on the shoulders of the bishops. . . . They think we should be excommunicating everybody who promotes abortion and that will take care of the problem. I don't think penalties solve problems."[68]

Pressure from Rome has attempted to stifle the efforts of Archbishop Rembert Weakland, who has been calling for more dialogue on the abortion issue. Conservative American Catholics have pressured Rome for stricter discipline. In a petition presented to U.S. pro-nuncio Archbishop Agostino Cacciavillan, the conservative organization Catholic Center accused Archbishop Weakland of a "pro-abortion betrayal of church teaching" and asked for action to "discipline this wayward pastor."[69]

After vetoing an honorary doctorate prepared for Weakland by the theological faculty of Switzerland's Fribourg University, the Vatican cited "confusion" brought on by Weakland's statements concerning the tactics of anti-abortion groups within the Church.[70] Weakland responded to the Vatican's actions by standing tough. "I can't imagine [being stopped] unless you take out my tongue," he said.[71] Other American bishops, however, while privately lauding Weakland, have been reluctant to publicly support him, fearing possible reprisal against themselves.[72]

DISCIPLINE OR PERSUASION

How to retain an influence over their followers has been the subject of much debate within the hierarchy. While some advocate sanctions and the enforcement of stricter discipline, others maintain that dialogue between the hierarchy and the laity should be emphasized to work out disputes. Archbishop Weakland flatly states his opposition to the heavy-handedness of disciplinarians: "I believe the model of confrontation, which [Cardinal O'Connor] espouses and which Rome seems to prefer, has become overworked and counterproductive."[73] In addition to Weakland, other American prelates opt for a more cooperative approach. Chicago's Cardinal Joseph Bernardin, in a carefully worded speech in March 1990, pointed out that "many Catholics, politicians and ordinary citizens, will disagree on strategies of implementation to lessen and prevent abortions." These matters, he stressed, "are open to debate."[74] In a similar vein, Sacramento Bishop Francis Quinn suggests that bishops face a related choice of strategy with regard to the subject of public controls over controversial and obscene material. Quinn stresses that a better approach would be to seek to change attitudes through moral persuasion rather than to use punitive sanctions.[75]

The debate over church political involvement is indicative of other tensions in the Church since the Second Vatican Council. The Church finds itself currently caught up in turmoil concerning its teachings and treatment of women and homosexuals. Unable to reconcile the Church's ban against women priests with its efforts to promote social and economic justice, American bishops in 1992 were forced to abandon a major pastoral letter on women in the Church.[76] Rising expectations of greater equality within the Roman Catholic Church run up against the Vatican's ban on the ordination of women. As Cardinal Bernardin stated, "In all honesty, we must admit that the central question which has emerged and is driving our discussion regarding the pastoral is that of the ordination of women."[77] Fearing an exodus from the Church like that seen after the issuance of *Humane vitae* in 1968, which banned the use of artificial birth control, Weakland argued that passage of the pastoral "would lose another generation, especially another generation of very wonderful women."[78]

In a similar struggle, the Church is grappling with its teaching and treatment of homosexuals. In contradiction to Vatican II and pastoral statements abhorring discrimination, a 1992 Vatican letter to United States bishops warned against civil laws protecting homosexuals from discrimination. "There are areas in which it is not unjust discrimination to take sexual orientation into account," it said. "For example, in the consignment of children to adoption or foster care, in employment of teachers or coaches, and in military recruitment."[79]

Several bishops, including Thomas Gumbleton, auxiliary bishop of Detroit; Walter Sullivan, bishop of Richmond, Virginia; and retired Bishop

Charles A. Buswell of Pueblo, Colorado, went on public record opposing the Vatican statement.[80] But many other bishops may be with them in spirit. A majority of the bishops responding to our survey (56 percent) disagree with the statement that "homosexuals should not teach in public schools." Similar polls of American Catholics have also found support for homosexual rights. According to a Gallup poll taken in the spring of 1992, 78 percent of U.S. Catholics favor equal job opportunities for gay people.[81] At a time when American Catholics and American bishops have become more supportive of equal job opportunities for homosexuals, the Vatican has intensified an already inflamed controversy.

These crises within the Church are by no means unusual. Throughout its history the Church struggled with conflicts between its religious leaders and the wider society. The context of current crises, however, can be traced back to the "promises" some Catholics believe were made at the Second Vatican Council but remain unfulfilled to this day. The profound religious and political changes over the last thirty years since the Council and the rising expectations of American Catholics have left Catholic leaders scrambling to maintain a meaningful political voice.

CONCLUSION

The simple classification themes common to the political development literature may not be completely suitable for explaining the current relationship between religion and politics. An assumption underlying many models is that religion remains static while political systems change. As modern systems advance, it is assumed, religion is left behind without contemporary relevance in the realm of politics. Religion is viewed as an impediment (or obsolete) to development in advanced societies. When religion no longer serves the purposes of government, it is argued, it is soon abandoned. But religion changes. Catholicism and its leaders have entered a new phase. Religion and politics are not on completely separate tracts. The interaction continues.

During the Middle Ages the Roman Catholic Church provided a source of authority necessary to orchestrate societal development. That authority was challenged not only by political leaders but by revolutions occurring in the realms of science and religion. The rise of the nation-states of Europe, the scientific revolution and the Enlightenment, and the Protestant Reformation all worked to end the dominance of the Roman Catholic Church.

But the Church found new ways to retain a role in politics. Taking advantage of its numbers, the Church mobilized new voters through political parties and interest groups. Once mobilized, however, the Church was presented a new task of exerting influence on the vote choices of its followers. The authoritarianism that served it well during the Middle Ages was no longer viable by the twentieth century. If the Church could not compel its followers by sanction, it would have to rely on the persuasiveness of its message. Affecting the hearts and minds of its people through moral persuasion required new approaches, many of which continue to be challenged by those who long for a return to a more "disciplined" Church.

While the Church no longer possesses the more direct influence on the state that it had during the Middle Ages, it has assumed a role as social critic and teacher of social morality. In seeking to teach social morality, American bishops hope to maintain a moral influence on political attitudes and beliefs. In this way religious leaders seek a part in the shaping of political culture. It is in this area that the religious influence on politics may have its greatest impact. But if the task of the modern church is to move the hearts and minds of its people, new strategies for bridging religion and political culture may be necessary. It is to an examination of this connection that we now turn.

NOTES

1. Guy Michelat and Michel Simon, "Religion, Class, and Politics," *Comparative Politics* 10, no. 1 (October 1977), p. 159.

2. Daniel Bell, "The Return of the Sacred? The Argument on the Future of Religion," *British Journal of Sociology* 28, no. 4 (December 1977), pp. 421–422.

3. Thomas Jefferson made this reference in a letter to the Danbury Baptist Association on January 1, 1802. In the Supreme Court's decision in *Everson*, Justice Black referred to Jefferson's comment in interpreting the establishment clause of the First Amendment. See *Everson v. Board of Education of the Township of Ewing*, 330 U.S. 1 (1947).

4. James A. Bill and Robert L. Hardgrave, Jr., *Comparative Politics: The Quest for Theory* (Lanham, Md.: University Press of America, 1981), p. 67.

5. See Alexander J. Groth, *Progress and Chaos: Modernization and Rediscovery of Religion and Authority* (Malabar, Fla.: Robert E. Kreiger, 1984), and Samuel P. Huntington, *Political Order in Changing Societies* (New Haven: Yale University Press, 1968).

6. Lucian W. Pye, *Aspects of Political Development* (Boston: Little, Brown, 1966), p. 38 and chap. 2.

7. Manfred Halpern, "Toward Further Modernization of the Study of New Nations," *World Politics* 17 (October 1964), p. 173.

8. Gabriel Almond and G. Bingham Powell, Jr., *Comparative Politics: A Developmental Approach* (Boston: Little, Brown, 1966), p. 105.

9. Donald Smith, *Religion and Political Development* (Boston: Little, Brown, 1970), p. 2.

10. See Fred W. Riggs, *Administration in Developing Countries: The Theory of Prismatic Society* (Boston: Houghton Mifflin, 1964).

11. See J. Milton Yinger, *The Scientific Study of Religion* (London: Macmillan, 1970), especially chap. 6.

12. Charles and Maclaren argue that the state needed this merge more than the church and for Catholicism it was a "mixed blessing." See Rodger Charles and Drostan Maclaren, *The Social Teaching of Vatican II: Its Origin and Development* (San Francisco: Ignatius Press, 1982), p. 20.

13. Thomas Renna, *Church and State in Medieval Europe 1050–1314* (Dubuque: Kendall/Hunt, 1974), p. 195. This connection between leadership and change is also stressed by Alfred Diamant. As he maintains, "Political development is a process by which a political system acquires an increased capacity to sustain successfully and continuously new types of goals and demands and the creation of new types of organizations." This often requires, however, centralized structures to "command resources from and power over wide spheres and regions of society." (See Alfred Diamant, "The Nature of Political Development," in Jason L. Finkle and Richard W. Gable, eds., *Political Development and Social Change* [New York: Wiley, 1966], p. 92.)

14. Quoted in Stephen Harding and David Phillips with Michael Fogarty, *Contrasting Values in Western Europe* (London: Macmillan, 1986), pp. 30–31.

15. Quoted in Thomas F. O'Dea, *The Catholic Crisis* (Boston: Beacon Press, 1968), p. 78.

16. Ibid.

17. See Renna, *Church and State in Medieval Europe*, chap. 1.

18. Donald Smith emphasizes the effects of these shifts in his statements that "(1) modernization in the West proceeded from a medieval synthesis of church integralism, and (2) the integralist medieval society was shattered by revolutionary pluralization in the religious and intellectual spheres." (See Smith, *Religion and Political Development*, p. 27.)

19. Quoted in Richard P. McBrien, *Catholicism* (Minneapolis: Winston Press, 1980), p. 643.

20. Third Plenary Council of Baltimore, "Pastoral Letter," December 7, 1884, in Hugh J. Nolan, ed., *Pastoral Letters of the United States Catholic Bishops*, vol.1 1792–1940 (Washington, D.C.: United States Catholic Conference, 1984), pp. 211–212.

21. Robert A. Nisbet, *Social Change and History* (New York: Oxford University Press, 1969), pp. 94–95.

22. See Michael Parenti, "Political Values and Religious Culture: Jews, Catholics and Protestants," *Journal for the Scientific Study of Religion* 6, no. 1 (Spring 1967), pp. 259–269.

23. Thomas O'Dea, *American Catholic Dilemma* (New York: Sheed and Ward, 1958).

24. Steven Ozment provides an insightful look into the effects of the Reformation in *Protestants: The Birth of a Revolution* (New York: Doubleday, 1992).

25. Peter Blickle, *Religion, Politics and Social Protest* (Boston: Allen and Unwin, 1984).

26. See Max Weber, *The Protestant Ethic and the Spirit of Capitalism*, trans. Talcott Parsons (New York: Scribner's, 1958). See also David D. Laitin, "Religion, Political Culture, and the Weberian Tradition," *World Politics* 30 (July 1978), pp. 563–592.

27. Quoted in John T. McNeill, ed., *Calvin: On God and Political Duty* (Indianapolis: Bobbs-Merrill, 1956), p. 53.

28. Ibid.

29. Perry Miller, *Errand into the Wilderness* (Cambridge, Mass.: Harvard University Press, 1956), p. 47.

30. John Cotton, *An Exposition upon the Thirteenth Chapter of the Revelation*, reprinted in part in Edmund S. Morgan, *Puritan Political Ideas* (Indianapolis: Bobbs-Merrill, 1965), p. 175.

31. Quoted in Henry Martyn Dexter, *The Congregationalism of the Last Three Hundred Years, as Seen in Its Literature: With Special Reference to Certain Recondite, Neglected, or Disputed Passages* (New York: Harper and Brothers, Publishers, 1880), p. 427.

32. Alan Heimert, *Religion and the American Mind* (Cambridge, Mass.: Harvard University Press, 1966), pp. 18–19.

33. Quoted in Morgan, *Puritan Political Ideas*, p. 313.

34. John Tracy Ellis, *American Catholicism*, 2nd ed. (Chicago: University of Chicago Press, 1969), p. 38.

35. Quoted in ibid., pp. 71–72.

36. Andrew M. Greeley, *The American Catholic: A Social Portrait* (New York: Basic Books, 1977), p. 20.

37. Henry Steele Commager, *The American Mind: An Interpretation of American Thought and Character since the 1880s* (New Haven: Yale University Press, 1950), p. 193.

38. Third Plenary Council of Baltimore, "Pastoral Letter," December 7, 1884, in Nolan, *Pastoral Letters*, p. 228.

39. See Thomas T. McAvoy, *The Great Crisis in American Catholic History 1895–1900* (Chicago: H. Regnery, 1957).

40. See William J. Gould, Jr., "The Challenge of Liberal Political Culture in the Thought of John Courtney Murray" (Paper presented at the 1990 Annual Meeting of the American Political Science Association, San Francisco, California).

41. See Robert D. Cross, *The Emergence of Liberal Catholicism in America* (Cambridge, Mass.: Harvard University Press, 1958).

42. Pope Pius X, *Pascendi dominici gregis*, 1907.

43. See Jay P. Dolan, *The American Catholic Experience: A History from Colonial Times to the Present* (Garden City, N.Y.: Doubleday, 1985), pp. 318–320.

44. See Vincent Yzermas, ed., *American Participation in the Second Vatican Council* (New York: Sheed and Ward, 1967).

45. John Tracy Ellis, "Religious Freedom: An American Reaction," in Alberic Stacpoole, ed., *Vatican II Revisited by Those who Were There* (Minneapolis: Winston Press, 1986), p. 294.

46. See John Courtney Murray, *We Hold These Truths* (New York: Sheed and Ward, 1960).

47. Aaron Seidman maintains that the lines of separation between the church and state in puritan society actually were evident earlier than this. "In spirit, in theory, and in practice, Massachusetts was not a church-dominated state, and . . . from the start, incipient seeds of the later complete division between church and state were already active," he argues. Seidman's main contention is that church intervention into politics often came after direct solicitation by secular leaders seeking help from church leaders to maintain their positions of authority. The fact that secular leaders depended upon the church authorities for their political survival, however, suggests that it would be wrong to argue that a separation between church and state existed to any great extent. See Aaron Seidman, "Church and State in the Early Years of the Massachusetts Bay Colony," *New England Quarterly* 18 (March-December 1945), p. 217.

48. See Gabriel Almond and Sidney Verba, *The Civic Culture* (Princeton: Princeton University Press, 1963).

49. Smith, *Religion and Political Development*, p. 124.

50. See Gianfranco Poggi, *Catholic Action in Italy* (Stanford: Stanford University Press, 1967).

51. Frederic Spotts, *The Churches and Politics in Germany* (Middletown, Conn.: Wesleyan University Press, 1973), p. 357.

52. Ibid., p. 355.

53. Quoted in Douglas A. Wertman, "The Catholic Church and Italian Politics: The Impact of Secularisation," in Suzanne Berger, ed., *Religion in West European Politics* (London: Frank Cass, 1982), p. 87.

54. See John H. Whyte, *Catholics in Western Democracies* (Dublin, Ireland: Gill and Macmillan, 1981), p. 89.

55. Quoted in ibid., p. 108.

56. Quoted in "The Church and Capitalism: A Report by Catholic Bishops on the U.S. Economy Will Cause a Furor," *Business Week*, November. 12, 1984, p. 105.

57. Timothy Byrnes argues that the American bishops were influenced most by political changes that encouraged them to become more politically active and that ambitious politicians sought to associate themselves with bishops for political advantage. See Timothy A. Byrnes, *Catholic Bishops in American Politics* (Princeton: Princeton University Press, 1991).

58. "Legislator Barred from Catholic Rite," *New York Times*, November 17, 1989, p. A11.

59. See "Cardinal Defends a Bishop in Clash with Cuomo," *New York Times*, February 1, 1990, p. A1.

60. "O'Connor Warns Politicians Risk Excommunication Over Abortion," *New York Times*, June 15, 1990, p. 1.

61. Despite instructions not to endorse or oppose candidates for public office or "engage in any partisan political activity," a conservative Catholic priest from Riverside, California, warned his congregation in 1992 that a vote for "pro-choice" Bill Clinton constituted a sin. The media attention this generated, however, is indicative of the rarity of such an action. See "Voting for Clinton Is Sin, Priest Says," *Los Angeles Times*, September 18, 1992, p. A3.

62. National Conference of Catholic Bishops, "The Challenge of Peace: God's Promise and Our Response" (Washington, D.C.: United States Catholic Conference, 1983), p. 101.

63. Quoted in *San Francisco Chronicle*, March 9, 1989, p. A4.

64. "Bishops Appear to Have Lost an Abortion Battle as Catholic Politicians March to a Secular Drum," *Wall Street Journal*, October 16, 1990, p. A32.

65. "Politicians Say Bishops' Pressure May Backfire," *Sacramento Bee*, December 8, 1989, p. A5.

66. Ibid.

67. One poll, for example, found 74 percent of Americans saying the bishops' political involvement in the abortion debate is improper. See "Bishops, Abortion No Mix, Poll Says," *San Jose Mercury News*, October 27, 1990, p. 10C.

68. Quoted in *National Catholic Reporter*, October 5, 1990, p. 3.

69. Ibid., p. 8.

70. See *National Catholic Reporter*, November 16, 1990, p. 1.

71. "Archbishop Defiant on Abortion Study," *San Jose Mercury News*, November 14, 1990, p. 8C.

72. See "The Irony of Bishops Seeking Cover of Secrecy," *National Catholic Reporter*, November 23, 1990, p. 20.

73. Quoted in *National Catholic Reporter*, January 8, 1993, p. 11.

74. "Cardinal Hints at Options for Politicians on Abortion," *New York Times*, March 21, 1990, p. A14.

75. See "Fight Obscenity with Education, Quinn Says," *National Catholic Reporter*, October 19, 1990, p. 4.

76. "Bishops Reject Pastoral Letter on Female Role," *Los Angeles Times*, November 19, 1992, p. A1.

77. Quoted in "Women's Pastoral Buried After 10 Years," *National Catholic Reporter* December 4, 1992, pp. 3–4.

78. Ibid., p. 4.

79. "Vatican Statement Supports Discrimination Against Gays," *Los Angeles Times*, July 17, 1992, p. A14.

80. "Three Bishops Join Opposition to Vatican Policy," *Los Angeles Times*, October 31, 1992, p. A24.

81. Cited in "Vatican Statement," *Los Angeles Times*, p. A14.

Chapter 3 _____

Religious Contributions to Political Culture

In addition to contributing to the development of political structures and institutions, religion influences public attitudes about government and politics that constitute a nation's political culture. Religious differences often account for cultural differences across and within societies. While the connection between religion and culture can be quite complex, religion is an integral source for the development of ideas and values that give meaning to the world and human life. A primary objective of the Second Vatican Council was for the Church to find new ways to apply religion to culture. Pope Paul VI stated in 1975 that "the split between the Gospel and culture is without a doubt the drama of our time, just as it was of other times. Therefore every effort must be made to ensure a full evangelization of culture, or more correctly of cultures."[1] The issuance of pastoral letters and the more active political involvement of United States Catholic bishops must be understood in light of Pope Paul's and the Second Vatican Council's call to cultural renewal.

On the connection between religion and culture, Paul Tillich argues that a solid bond exists: "Religion as ultimate concern is the meaning-giving substance of culture, and culture is the totality of forms in which the basic concern of religion expresses itself; religion is the substance of culture, culture is the form of religion."[2] While Tillich may overstate the relationship between religion and culture, particularly given the secularizing tendencies within society, religion often provides a powerful belief system upon which values are nourished and culture is established. These values can be expected to affect political beliefs as well.

The concept of political culture, which was adapted from anthropology, was first introduced in the study of politics by Gabriel Almond in his article "Comparative Political Systems."[3] Almond used the term to refer to "specifically political orientations—attitudes toward the political system and its various parts, and attitudes toward the role of the self in the system."[4] Sidney Verba, a collaborator with Almond, elaborated that political culture is "the system of empirical beliefs, expressive symbols, and values which define the situation in which political action takes place. It provides the subjective orientation to politics."[5] For Lucian Pye, "Political culture is the set of attitudes, beliefs, and sentiments which give order and meaning to a political process and which provide the underlying assumptions and rules that govern behavior in the political system."[6] In essence, the collective political values held by a nation's people constitute the political culture.

Widely shared values can contribute to a dominant political culture, but when differing values are present, a variety of separate political subcultures may be present in one society. Almond and Powell emphasize the "underlying propensities" within political systems and the existence of subcultures within societies. In defining political culture, they conclude that "it consists of attitudes, beliefs, values, and skills which are current in an entire population, as well as those special propensities and patterns which may be found within separate parts of that population."[7] When there is wide agreement on the basic ground rules of politics, stability is more readily sustained. Where deep disagreement over basic political values is evident, revolutions, civil wars, and frequent government turnovers are more likely.

Measuring and defining the dimensions of political values and beliefs, however, can be problematic. The use of political culture as an explanatory variable has been questioned on several counts. James Bill and Robert Hardgrave suggest that the approach "remains tautological, generally failing to distinguish analytically its use as either a dependent or independent variable vis-à-vis the political system. It does not provide the analytical capacity to explain why political systems evolve as they do or why they differ."[8] In other words, does the existence of a particular political system lead to a general acceptance by the people, or must certain political values already be present before a system can develop? This question has no easy answer. While attitudes toward the role of government prompted America's founders to establish a constitution that greatly limits the power of the state, the American preference for pragmatic rather than ideological government is reinforced by the realities of the political system.

Others worry that if the concept of political culture is not narrowly defined, it can be stretched so far that it merely becomes "a depository for data and findings that cannot be covered by other labels."9

These criticisms are fair ones. Because of the somewhat amorphous nature of political (as well as religious) values, the cultural approach to the study of politics does not always lend itself easily to quantitative measurement. But this is not to say that the concept is therefore not useful. When it is recognized that political culture is more than merely an explanatory variable of behavior, and that its dynamic dimension can account for political change as well, the utility of the concept is magnified. Political values change just as political systems change. As levels of education and economic status rise, so also may a person's outlook on the world.

In their classic work *Civic Culture*, Almond and Verba identify several sources for the development of political cultures. While education, which fosters political tolerance and a participatory culture, is ranked high on their list, they also stress the need for "unifying symbols," "social trust," and "civic cooperativeness."10 The degree to which one has trust in the political system or possesses a desire to participate in the system is tied to questions of system legitimacy and personal obligation. If the system is viewed as moral and citizens feel a duty or moral obligation to contribute to the community, a participatory culture is more likely to develop. To the extent that religion often serves as a basis for morality, the elements of the "civic culture" often have roots in religion.

A shared system of beliefs and practices can serve to promote a sense of social solidarity and civic cooperativeness. When religion provides a moral framework from which to judge the legitimacy of a political system, it can serve as further justification for the established order. Where religious differences contribute to social division, however, religious subcultures can also work to divide a political commmunity. The basis of monarchical authority justified by a "divine right" of kings was legitimized by the sanction of the dominant Roman Catholic Church. As the Church lost its position as the primary religious authority, new religious theologies and sects developed that could justify different political arrangements.

RELIGION AS A SOURCE OF CULTURAL STABILITY

Political culture (or a value structure) is a glue that can hold society together. When there is congruence between value and structure, stability can be fostered.[11] Medieval church theology stressed the order and stability in God's creation. Church teaching on the perfection and order in God's creation was conducive to political values that emphasized order and hierarchy in politics. So long as individuals accepted hierarchical political authority as legitimate, stability was sustained.

While religion can be a contributing force, the maintenance of order and stability can be secured in other ways as well. According to Hobbes, due to the selfishness of men and the potential chaos in the state of nature, an absolute ruler is necessary to ensure order and stability.[12] Karl Marx and other coercion theorists point to the unequal distribution of property as the source of instability in society. A capitalist elite secures its position of power by infusing its values throughout the system, often through coercion. Focusing on the inequality inherent in most social organizations, Ralf Dahrendorf argues that "the fundamental inequality of social structure, and the lasting determinant of social conflict, is the inequality of power and authority which inevitably accompanies social organization."[13] Further, he maintains that "from the point of view of coercion theory it is not voluntary cooperation or general consensus but enforced constraint that makes social organizations cohere."[14]

In democratic systems, however, "enforced constraint" is rarely viable. Where individual freedom is guaranteed, societal stability is maintained when there is a congruence between the moral values of the citizenry and the perceived performance of the system. When performance falls short of lofty ideals, however, threats to stability become increasingly evident.[15]

Hierarchical church authority and the use of sanctions including excommunication illustrate the potential for religious coercion. While one could point to the tactics of the crusaders and church inquisitions as examples of coercive attempts on the part of religion (aligned with the state) to maintain control, in modern democratic systems the Church no longer can sustain such a position of power. When the Church lost its ability to use coercion, its influence rested in the power of its teaching message.

Church theology and social teaching offer a framework through which to view the world. In this sense, religion can provide a kind of moral legitimacy to government. As the Western world moved toward democracy, religion could be used to justify the principles upon which the system rested. Agreement on fundamental principles and political ground rules is essential to the maintenance of a stable democracy. Without moral controls, military power would dominate. Without moral principles, there would be no "right" outside of "might."

The church emphasis that man is ultimately responsible to a power higher than the state offers a transcendent support for justice. Carl Friedrich maintains that the development of constitutional government "must be understood as embedded in the belief system of Western Christianity and the political thought that expresses its implications for the secular order."[16] Hegel attributes to Lutheran Protestantism a large influence in the development of secular freedom. Lutheranism, he argues, promoted "a sentiment which . . . is the foundation of all the equitable arrangements that prevail with regard to private right and the constitution of the state."[17]

The place of religion in a morally based society has been emphasized in the works of many political theorists. According to Montesquieu, "He who has no religion at all is that terrible animal who perceives his liberty only when he tears in pieces and when he devours."[18] For the maintenance of order, Hegel points out that "it is in being . . . related to religion that state, laws, and duties all alike acquire for consciousness their supreme confirmation and their supreme obligatoriness, because . . . in religion there lies the place where man is always assured of finding a consciousness of the unchangeable, of the highest freedom and satisfaction."[19] Even Machiavelli suggested that "princes and republics who wish to maintain themselves free from corruption must above all things preserve the purity of all religious observances, and treat them with proper reverence; for there is no greater indication of the ruin of a country than to see religion condemned."[20]

RELIGION AND THE AMERICAN REPUBLIC

America's founders emphasized the importance of civic virtue to republican government. Their republican ideals included the hope for a virtuous society. As Gordon Wood puts it, "There was, the eighteenth century believed, a reciprocating relationship between the structure of the government and the spirit of its people."[21] John Adams defended a republican constitution because it "introduces knowledge among the people, and inspires them with a conscious dignity becoming freemen. . . . That elevation of sentiment inspired by such a government, makes the common people brave and enterprising. That ambition which is inspired by it makes them sober, industrious, and frugal."[22] Not only is a republic necessary to check tyranny, it facilitates the education of a responsible and virtuous people.

Puritan views of government in general, and those reflected in puritan practices, closely resemble the republican principles that would be the basis for revolution and the creation of the new government of 1789. Though the source of puritan political thought stemmed primarily from its theology, the infiltration of secular ideas and influences would transform puritan politics into republicanism.

Puritan views of human nature and of man's relationship with God served as the underpinnings for a reticent support for democratic tendencies in government. Man's sinful nature was viewed as an obstacle to pure democracy, and yet the need to check tyranny required some form of democracy. American Protestantism also recognized the importance of government in keeping men moral. The commonwealth of covenanted individuals contributing to the public good promised a virtuous people. This belief buttressed the optimism of the founders and generations of Americans to come.[23]

While one would be hard-pressed to argue that religion alone shaped the political values of early America, the deep attachment Americans have had to their religious values has spilled over into many aspects of their lives. The rhetoric, symbols, and myths used by the founders (men who were not overtly religious) reflected those of federalist clergy.[24] Presidents throughout American history have used religious rhetoric and symbols to embolden their political causes.[25] And the religious beliefs of candidates for the office have been the subject of much scrutiny.[26] Many presidents have recognized the political salience of religion in justifying political action. The Bush administration's attempt to place the Persian Gulf war in the context of "just war" theory attests to the impact the American bishops' pastoral letter "Challenge of Peace" has had in influencing the public debate.

So important is the need for a moral justification for society that, absent a religious basis, some have maintained that a form of civil religion has replaced, or should replace, traditional religion as a source of political legitimacy. Rousseau was the first to use the term "civil religion." While he maintained that "no state has ever been founded without religion as its base," he was not convinced of the utility of building a society on Christian tenets.[27] "Christianity," he argued, "preaches only servitude and submission. Its spirit is too favourable to tyranny for tyranny not to take advantage of it."[28] But in its place, he pointed out the importance of a "profession of faith which is purely civil and of which it is the sovereign's function to determine the articles, not strictly as religious dogmas, but as sentiments of sociability, without which it is impossible to be either a good citizen or a loyal subject."[29] Political morality and a sense of political obligation must be nurtured. They are not inherent human traits.

While shared political values have their roots in a variety of sources, in contrast, religion is a natural antecedent. Religion offers an already established, unified set of beliefs. Religious values are included with many of a person's earliest learned principles of behavior. They are deeply ingrained and offer a natural basis upon which one views other aspects of the world.

RELIGION AND POLITICAL SOCIALIZATION

How we learn religious (and political) values depends upon a process of socialization, or social learning. Variable processes of political socialization work to orient religious subgroups differently toward politics. Individuals are strongly influenced by the values and norms of groups with which they associate.[30] The most important primary group is the family. Attitudes toward the system of government and trust in government are transmitted through families to successive generations. In families where politics is viewed negatively, such attitudes are often taken on by the children.

In a study of French socialization, Annick Percheron finds that "regardless of social group, educational level or the parent's gender, religion is better transmitted than politics."[31] In French households politics is not commonly discussed. Particularly in the households of practicing Catholics, "politics is something that the family is reluctant to discuss, and ideological preferences are transmitted despite the educational ideals affirmed by most parents. Three principles form the basis of parents' attitudes: childhood and politics should not be mixed; religion and politics should not be mixed; and, a fortiori, childhood, religion and politics should not be mixed."[32] Catholic families on the Left, however, are more likely to emphasize politics and socialize their children to be politically active. In families where religion is not so important, the transmission of political values is even more direct. "Along with regular church-going Catholics on the Left, but far ahead of them, the irreligious are those who have the most coherent value system and who best succeed in passing it onto their descendants, even without the support of any specific institution."[33] So important is early socialization that a later decline in church attendance among practicing Catholics does not necessarily lead one to the political Left.

This is not to say that Catholics are always nonpolitical or supporters of the political Right. When they are socialized on the political Left, distinct Catholic left-wing cultures exist in France. Jean-Marie Donegani differentiates between political subcultures of French Catholics.[34] While those Catholics who are considered practicing because of frequency of church attendance are overwhelmingly supportive of the political Right, Donegani maintains that a significant Catholic Left movement exists.

These Catholic leftists can be found in Catholic Action movements that have become increasingly politicized. While many of these groups do not enjoy the blessings of the Catholic hierarchy, members feel a commitment to their religious interpretation of Catholicism. French Catholics challenging the institutions of the French Catholic Church are often likely to hold negative attitudes about the institutions of government as well.[35]

The development of religiopolitical subcultures has been quite marked in Dutch society as well. The "pillarisation" of society on religious grounds has contributed to distinct cultural subgroups. "Pillarisation in the Netherlands may be described as the situation in which people's lives, from childhood to old age, are organised on the basis of religion (particularly Catholicism and Protestantism)."[36] Thung and colleagues maintain that there have been at least three cultural subgroups in the Netherlands since the Reformation: a liberal-humanist, an orthodox-Calvinist, and a Catholic group.[37] These groups have shown distinct political behaviors, often bitterly in opposition to one another. Fortunately, for the stability of the regime, a "politics of accommodation" has allowed the elites of the several pillars to govern while keeping their followers apart.[38]

Irish political culture, on the other hand, has been marked by a relative homogeneity (Northern Ireland excepted). In a country where overwhelming majorities are practicing Catholics, subcultures are not as prevelant. Strong Catholic influence in Irish families helps to maintain a dominant religious culture. Religion, however, works to foster stable and widely accepted political attitudes. So strong is this unifying force in Ireland that even class conflicts are uncommon. A commonality in religious attachments has overshadowed potentially dividing cleavages.

In the United States the multiplicity of religious sects and values has contributed to a variety of distinct political subcultures. Historians, including Louis Hartz and Daniel Boorstin, argue that America's unique liberal culture has shaped the way Americans view politics and behave politically. Beliefs in the virtue of limited government and personal freedom influence individual and collective political attitudes and behavior.[39] McClosky and Zaller show that Americans continue to harbor ambivalent attitudes about capitalism and democracy and this ambivalence has profound impact on the political process and institutions.[40] These attitudes, though widely shared, are held in varying intensities. As a result of somewhat distinct political and cultural histories, Americans are not homogeneous. Tapping these subcultural differences is crucial to the understanding of American culture.

CATHOLIC CONTRIBUTIONS

Catholic contributions to American political culture have been minimized by those who stress the acculturation of Catholics into the predominantly Protestant American society. In some respects American Catholicism is more "Protestant" than the Catholicism found in Europe. As Henry J. Browne argues, American Catholics "know that they and their predecessors have to some extent carried their beliefs into education and industry and other avenues of life, even into the field of entertainment. But they have much more often conformed to values than changed them."[41] Martin Marty describes this as the "Americanization of Catholicism."[42]

This "Americanization" includes support for the liberal democratic tradition. Individualism and ambivalence toward authority have been characteristics shared by Americans, Catholic and Protestant.[43] One anonymous bishop who responded to our survey, commenting on Americans' independent thinking with regard to the bishops' social and political statements, lamented, "I'm not convinced of our hearing from the public, both Catholic and non. I am convinced that many, many Catholics—like many Protestants—are more American than Catholic (Protestant)." As Cardinal Bernardin explained to Pope John Paul II in 1989, "Americans are accustomed to government in the open" and "to exercising their basic freedoms by civil discourse, open to inquiry into any issue. . . . As a faith community, we operate according to different principles, both in terms of our teaching and governance."[44]

Nevertheless, while American Catholics share many similarities with their Protestant counterparts, Catholics are different in important ways. While widely shared societal values contribute to bridging the gap between Catholics and Protestants, political differences are evident (see chapter 6). These differences can be attributed to upbringings in differing cultural and religious settings. The socialization process extends beyond the family and is affected by group affiliations.

THE CHURCH AS POLITICAL COMMUNITY

The notion of a "moral community" giving legitimacy to social and political action has been stresssed in the works of Parsons and Durkheim. For them, political cultures (or values) are derived from communities of believers. According to Parsons, the "integration of a set of common value patterns with the internalized need disposition structure of the constituent personalities [i.e., sane, socialized people playing roles in the system] is the core phenomenon of the dynamics of social systems."[45] A social system implies an interconnection between individuals who work toward common goals and objectives. Those brought together in the moral community of a church find a similarity of beliefs and goals. Brought to the political realm, this solidarity can provide a basis for civic cooperativeness.

In *Elementary Forms of the Religious Life*, Emile Durkheim defines religion as "a unified system of beliefs and practices relative to sacred things . . . beliefs and practices which unite into one single moral community . . . all those who adhere to them."[46] These shared beliefs and practices help to shape the interaction between the individual and society. They work to establish a social identity and define one's proper behavior within society.

In nineteenth-century France, the Catholic Church promoted the claims of miracles, apparitions, Marian devotion, and the pilgrimages to shrines to help nourish a closer attachment between the people and the Church. According to Thomas Kselman:

While miracle cults evoked nostalgic memories of a mythic past of uniform belief, they also offered an alternative to it. The community of belief was no longer to be the neighborhood or the village: it was expanded to include all of France, or at least all those of France who shared similar religious convictions. National confraternities, organized pilgrimages, and the diffusion of mass-produced images and literature were an attempt to use miracles to help create a sense of loyalty to French Catholicism, and beyond that, to the universal Church.[47]

Religious ritual and unifying symbols together can help to nurture the development and maintenance of a sense of community that depends upon shared experience. Sharing in religious ritual serves as a primary source of interaction to nurture communal affect.[48] David Martin argues that Catholic iconography provides a "conscience of collective."[49]

The religious community also offers parishioners many opportunities to learn political skills and serves as an outlet in which to practice politics. Religious ideas offer a "source of commitment and motivation."[50] Priests and bishops extolling the public manifestations of faith from the pulpit may serve as a source of inspiration for parishioners. But the parish itself serves as a natural political organization for communicating ideas and coordinating action. Many Catholic parishes have peace and justice groups, pro-life groups, and organizations like the St. Vincent de Paul Society, which serves as a church social welfare organization. In these environments church members are exposed to the political ideas of others.

These organizations serve as informal schools for learning more about politics from a religious perspective.

This view of church as a community is popular among Catholics. In the Notre Dame Study of Catholic Parish Life, when Catholics were given a choice of possible images of church, the most preferred (by 42 percent) was that of the church as "the community of believers."[51] In another study, Dixon and Hoge found that the most preferred view of the church was that of a "mystical communion," or community of believers.[52] Given the communal emphasis within the church, opportunities for cooperative efforts, interchanges of ideas, and, therefore, group socialization are more possible than in an environment in which religious action is primarily personal.

Wald, Owen, and Hill demonstrate the importance of viewing churches as political communities. They find strong correlations between the theological emphasis of a church and the political attitudes of its members. "The extent of theological traditionalism prevailing in the congregation moves individual members to more conservative preferences on social issues and makes them more disposed to identify as political conservatives."[53] This connection between theological and political views is an important, though infrequently studied, phenomenon. The authors rightfully stress a need to "redirect inquiry on religion and politics from an individualist perpective toward models that stress the formative influence of the immediate religious environment."[54]

CONCLUSION

While each congregation is unique, all Catholic parishes follow the same order of the Mass, and they share in a church teaching that is transmitted from higher authorities within the Church. More so than Protestant congregations, Catholic parishes are more directly responsive to the influence of a church hierarchy. All parishes and priests within a diocese are answerable to the bishop. A program of reform, therefore, if vigorously pushed by church leaders, has a good chance of percolating into the lives of practicing Catholics.

Over the last several decades, that formative environment of the church has been transformed by a theological revolution within Roman Catholicism. We now turn to an examination of this event, the Second Vatican Council.

NOTES

1. Quoted in Herve Carrier, "Understanding Culture: The Ultimate Challenge of the World-Church?" in Joseph Gremillion, ed., *The Church and Culture since Vatican II: The Experience of North and Latin America* (Notre Dame, Ind.: University of Notre Dame Press, 1985), p. 20.

2. Paul Tillich, *Theology of Culture* (Oxford, England: Oxford University Press, 1964), p. 42.

3. Gabriel A. Almond, "Comparative Political Systems," *Journal of Politics* 18, no. 3 (August 1956), pp. 391–409.

4. Gabriel Almond and Sidney Verba, *The Civic Culture* (Princeton: Princeton University Press, 1963), p. 13.

5. Sidney Verba, "Comparative Political Culture," in Lucian Pye and Sidney Verba, eds., *Political Culture and Political Development* (Princeton: Princeton University Press, 1965), p. 513.

6. Lucian Pye, "Political Culture," *International Encyclopedia of the Social Sciences*, vol. 12, (New York: Macmillan and Free Press, 1968) p. 218.

7. Gabriel A. Almond and G. Bingham Powell, Jr., *Comparative Politics: A Developmental Approach* (Boston: Little, Brown, 1966), p. 23.

8. James A. Bill and Robert L. Hardgrave, Jr., *Comparative Politics: The Quest for Theory* (Lanham, Md.: University Press of America, 1981), p. 114.

9. Alan Rosenthal, "On Analyzing States," in Alan Rosenthal and Maureen Moakley, eds., *The Political Life of the American States* (New York: Praeger, 1984), p. 11.

10. See Almond and Verba, *The Civic Culture*, p. 501.

11. See, for example, Almond and Verba, *The Civic Culture*, and Chalmers Johnson, *Revolutionary Change* (Boston: Little, Brown, 1966).

12. Thomas Hobbes, *The Leviathan* (Cambridge, England: Cambridge University Press, 1990).

13. Ralf Dahrendorf, *Class and Class Conflict in Industrial Society* (Stanford: Stanford University Press, 1959), p. 64.

14. Ibid., pp. 30–31.

15. See Samuel Huntington, *American Politics: The Promise of Disharmony* (Cambridge, Mass.: Belknap Press, 1981).

16. See Carl J. Friedrich, *Transcendent Justice: The Religious Foundations of Constitutionalism* (Durham, N.C.: Duke University Press, 1964), p. 3.

17. G.F.W. Hegel, *The Philosophy of History*, trans. J. Sibree (New York: Willey Book Co., 1956), p. 144.

18. Charles-Louis de Secondat Montesquieu, *The Spirit of the Laws*, vols. 2, 24, trans. Thomas Nugent (New York: Hafner, 1949), p. 28.

19. G.W.F. Hegel, *The Philosophy of Right*, trans. T. M. Knox (London: Oxford University Press, 1967), p. 166.

20. Niccolò Machiavelli, *Discourses*, bk. 1, chap. 12, in Max Lerner, ed., *The Prince and the Discourses* (New York: The Modern Library, 1950), p. 149.

21. Gordon S. Wood, *The Creation of the American Republic* (Williamsburg, Va.: Institute of Early American History and Culture, 1969), p. 119.

22. Quoted in ibid.

23. See Garry Wills, *Under God: Religion and American Politics* (New York: Simon and Schuster, 1990).

24. See Harry S. Stout, "Rhetoric and Reality in the Early Republic: The Case of the Federalist Clergy," in Mark A. Noll, ed., *Religion and American Politics: From the Colonial Period to the 1980s* (New York: Oxford University Press, 1990).

25. Edmund Fuller, *God in the White House: The Faiths of American Presidents* (New York: Crown, 1968).

26. Kenneth D. Wald, *Religion and Politics in the United States* (New York: St. Martin's Press, 1987), pp. 163–166.

27. Jean-Jacques Rousseau, *The Social Contract*, trans. Maurice Cranston (New York: Penguin Books, 1968), bk. 4, chap. 8, p. 180.

28. Ibid., p. 184.

29. Ibid., p. 186.

30. See Pamela Johnston Conover, "The Influence of Group Identification on Political Perception and Evaluation," *Journal of Politics* 46, no. 3 (August 1984), pp. 760–785, and Henry E. Brady and Paul M. Sniderman, "Attitude Attribution: A Group Basis for Political Reasoning," *American Political Science Review* 79, no. 4 (December 1985), pp. 1061–1078.

31. Annick Percheron, "Religious Acculturation and Political Socialisation in France," in Suzanne Berger, ed., *Religion in West European Politics* (London: Frank Cass, 1983), p. 13.

32. Ibid., p. 17.

33. Ibid., p. 29.

34. Jean-Marie Donegani, "The Political Cultures of French Catholicism," in Berger, *Religion in West European Politics*, p. 13.

35. See Renaud Dulong, "Christian Militants in the French Left," in Berger, *Religion in West European Politics*.

36. Mady A. Thung, Gert J. Peelen, and Marten C. Kingmans, "Dutch Pillarisation on the Move? Political Destabilisation and Religious Change," in Berger, *Religion in West European Politics*, p. 127.

37. For a history of the development of these groups see ibid.

38. See Arend Lijphart, *The Politics of Accommodation: Pluralism and Democracy in the Netherlands* (Berkeley: University of California Press, 1968).

39. Daniel Boorstin, *The Genius of American Politics* (Chicago: University of Chicago Press, 1953), and Louis Hartz, *The Liberal Tradition in America* (New York: Harcourt, Brace, 1955).

40. Herbert McClosky and John Zaller, *The American Ethos: Public Attitudes toward Capitalism and Democracy* (Cambridge, Mass.: Harvard University Press, 1984). See also Robert N. Bellah, Richard Madsen, William M. Sullivan, Ann Swidler, and Steven M. Tipton, *Habits of the Heart* (New York: Harper and Row, 1985), especially chap. 11.

41. Quoted in John Tracy Ellis, *American Catholicism*, 2nd ed. (Chicago: University of Chicago Press, 1969), p. 252.

42. Martin Marty, *Religion and Republic: The American Circumstance* (Boston: Beacon Press, 1987), pp. 182–183.

43. See, for example, Bellah et al., *Habits of the Heart*.

44. Quoted in *San Francisco Chronicle*, March 9, 1989, p. A4.

45. Talcott Parsons, *The Social System* (New York: Free Press, 1964), p. 42.

46. Emile Durkheim, *The Elementary Forms of the Religious Life*, trans. Joseph Ward Swain (New York: Free Press, 1965), p. 97.

47. Thomas Kselman, *Miracles and Prophecies in Nineteenth-Century France* (New Brunswick: Rutgers University Press, 1983), p. 199.

48. See Cynthia Toolin, "American Civil Religion from 1789–1981," *Review of Religious Research* 25, no. 1 (September 1983), pp. 39–48.

49. David Martin, "Religion and Public Values: A Catholic-Protestant Contrast," *Review of Religious Research* 26, no. 4 (June 1985), p. 313.

50. Wald, *Religion and Politics*, pp. 29–33.

51. David C. Leege and Thomas A. Trozzolo, "Religious Values and Parish Participation: The Paradox of Individual Needs in a Communitarian Church." Notre Dame Study of Catholic Parish Life, no. 4, June 1985, pp. 1–8.

52. Robert Dixon and Dean Hoge, "Models and Priorities of the Catholic Church as Held by Suburban Laity," *Review of Religious Research* 20, no. 2 (Spring 1979), pp. 150–167.

53. Kenneth D. Wald, Dennis E. Owen, and Samuel S. Hill, Jr., "Churches and Political Communities," *American Political Sceince Review* 82, no. 2 (June 1988), p. 543.

54. Ibid., p. 545.

Chapter 4 _____

Catholic Social Teaching and the
Second Vatican Council

On October 11, 1962, more than two thousand Roman Catholic bishops, cardinals, and other members of the hierarchy assembled in Rome for the Second Vatican Council. This extraordinary event, which lasted three years, would lead to profound changes within the Church. For many Catholics, Vatican II is best known for its reforms to change the Latin Mass and to lift the Friday meat ban. But more profoundly, the Council attempted to reshape the place of the Church in society. The Council offered a reconsideration of church law and policy concerning a wide variety of areas including religious life, the Mass, and the place of the Church in a rapidly modernizing world. While the documents were not intended to be political, reappraisal of its place in society forced the Church to reconsider the Catholic role in politics. The call from the Council was for more active engagement with the world to help improve the human condition. By the mid-twentieth century, the Church finally recognized that it had to adjust.

The message of Vatican II signified a major shift in the Church, away from a static worldview. A contest between conservatives, who tend to view religion in abstract, ahistorical terms, and those who see religion as evolving through history has long existed within the Church.[1] At the Second Vatican Council, however, the latter view was applied to the development of Catholic social teaching. According to theologian Charles Curran, the "shift that occurred in Catholic social teaching was from classicism to a historical consciousness. Classicism talked about the eternal, the immutable, the unchanging tendencies, using deductive methodology. Historical consciousness gave more importance to the particular, the individual, the contingent, the changing, the historical."[2] The reactions of the Church toward the Reformation, the scientific revolution, and modernization stemmed from the old view of the Church as a protector of immutable truths. Rigid authoritarianism was seen as necessary to bolster the position of those "truths" in the face of attacks. The Second Vatican Council, however, sought to get back to the biblical notion of God working through historical change.

THE SURPRISE ANNOUNCEMENT

In January 1959 the recently elected Pope John XXIII surprised the world when he announced his call for a Second Vatican Council.[3] For those who viewed the Church as monolithically controlled by the papacy, the First Vatican Council (1869–1870) seemed to negate a need for ecumenical councils. Vatican I led to the doctrine of papal primacy and infallibility. Why, then, would a pontiff feel compelled to consult with all of his bishops when declaring dogmatic truths?

Catholic leaders were also surprised by the suddenness of John's decision. They knew that popes rarely make such important decisions without first seeking wide consultation with other church leaders and close advisors.[4] As Pope John admitted, he was also surprised by the suddenness in which the idea came to him: "Suddenly and unexpectedly we were struck, as it were, by thought of this, within the lowliness of our spirit . . . [I]t sprang or had sprung up with us as does the first flower of an early springtime."[5]

What could the pope have in mind? Why call an ecumenical council at this time?[6] Every other ecumenical council in church history had been called to deal with a major crisis or settle a major doctrinal dispute. The Council of Nicea in 325 was called to settle the Arian heresy. Arius, a priest from Alexandria, questioned whether Jesus was really God. At Nicea the council exclaimed the divinity of Jesus as a dogma of the Church. The Council of Trent (1545–1563) was called to confront Protestant attacks on the Church that emanated from the Reformation. Vatican I (1869–1870) asserted the primacy and infallibility of the pope in the face of perceived secular and religious challenges to the papacy. Vatican II, however, was the first ecumenical council not called in a time of major church crisis.

The Council was not called to settle disputed doctrine, but to reconcile Christianity with the modern world, to bring about an aggiornamento, or updating of the Church. "The salient point of this Council," Pope John stated, "is not . . . a discussion of one article or another of the fundamental doctrine of the Church." Rather, finding a more effective way to make church teaching relevant in the modern world required that that doctrine "should be studied and expounded through modern research and modern scholarly disciplines."[7] Reconciling religious beliefs with modern science required an updating of church doctrine and the development of new techniques for teaching the Gospel message.[8]

The new approach emphasized a need for the Church to educate by demonstrating the persuasiveness of its teaching rather than using authoritarian sanctions. Pope John maintained that "the spouse of Christ prefers to make use of the medicine of mercy rather than that of severity. She considers that she meets the needs of the present day by demonstrating the validity of her teaching rather than by condemnations."[9] Threats and sanctions had become outmoded. New tactics were necessary.

This view was similarly held by John XXIII's successor. While John gave initial inspiration to the Council, it was his successor who brought the Church through its major transition. When Cardinal Montini was elected Pope Paul VI in 1963 the world wondered if he would quickly wrap up the Council or continue in John's path. But Pope Paul VI embraced the Council spirit and saw it through to its fruition and end on December 8, 1965.

Like John XXIII, Pope Paul VI viewed the Council as a renewal necessary to bring the Church into the modern world. In January 1963, Paul (then Cardinal Montini) summarized his view of Vatican II:

At the Council, the Church is looking for itself. It is trying, with great trust and with a great effort, to define itself more precisely and to understand what it is. After twenty centuries of history, the Church seems to be submerged by profane civilization and to be absent from the contemporary world. It is therefore experiencing the need to be recollected and to purify and recover itself so as to be able to set off on its own path again with great energy. . . . While it is undertaking the task of defining itself in this way, the Church is also looking for the world and trying to come into contact with that society. . . . How should that contact be established? By engaging in dialogue with the world, interpreting the needs of the society in which it is working and observing the defects, the necessities, the sufferings and the hopes and aspirations that exist in men's hearts.[10]

According to Paul, the Church must embrace the world rather than distance itself from it. For the Church to grow, it would need to utilize the expert knowledge and contributions offered by the laity and non-Catholics. It would need to accept the inevitability of its historical journey, striving to adapt and grow along with its people.

A DIFFERENT COUNCIL

Vatican II stands out from past ecumenical councils in several ways. By addressing the need to reconcile the Church with the world, the Council was the only ecumenical council in church history to address the temporal order in its formal agenda. It also developed the first council document in history devoted solely to the role of the laity in the Church. By defining the collegial authority of bishops the Council greatly boosted the position of bishops within the church hierarchy. And for the first time it was admitted that salvation is possible outside of the Catholic Church. This signified a major departure from the view of Pope Boniface VIII, who declared in the bull *Unam sanctam* in 1302 that "there is one holy catholic and apostolic Church, outside of which there is neither salvation nor remission of sins."[11] A declaration on religious liberty and calls for ecumenical collaboration with other religions signified an effort toward reconciliation with former religious enemies.

While these reforms were undertaken for a variety of nonpolitical reasons, their impact on American politics has been extensive. The emphasis on the collegiality of bishops and the call for the establishment of national episcopal conferences encouraged American Catholic bishops to increase their level of involvement in the political debate. The bishops' politics is based heavily on the political and social teachings of the Council. Ecumenism and an endorsement of religious freedom gave sanction to the American ideal of separation of church and state and would lay the groundwork for collaborative political action between Catholics and Protestants in the pro-life and peace movements in the United States. Encouragement of a greater role for the laity in the Church and an emphasis on the importance of personal conscience gave justification for the development of an invigorated sense of religious independence among Catholics. All of these changes worked to deemphasize the authoritarian aspects of Catholicism and to make the Church more truly catholic. The Council's definition of the Church as "the People of God" rather than an institution of rules and authority figures marks a shift from a tradition emphasized by Pope Gregory XVI (1831–1846). According to Gregory, "No one can overlook the fact that the Church is an unequal society in which God has destined some to command and others to obey. The latter are the laity, while the former are the clergy."[12] By elevating the role of lay persons, however, Vatican II sought to bridge the gap between clergy and laity.

Pope Paul VI chose to downplay differences between people. "The World will not be saved from outside," he said. "Without claiming privileges that will put us at a distance from others, without preserving the barrier of an incomprehensible language, we have to share the customs that are common to all. . . . We have to become brothers of our fellow-men."[13] Reconciliation among the peoples of the world and a recognition of alternative approaches to problem solving signify the mission of the Church as the People of God. Support for improved social arrangements, religious tolerance, and political pluralism rather than rigid authoritarianism mark the Vatican II spirit.

CHURCH AND STATE

The Council's position on questions of church-state relations also differed from that of earlier popes, who maintained that the Church was superior to the political order and therefore should be allowed to seek protection from the state. The tone of the Council is in stark contrast to the words of Pope Leo XIII, who argued that "all public power must proceed from God,"[14] and that "the State, constituted as it is, is clearly bound to act up to the manifold duties linking it to God, by the public profession of religion."[15] With respect to the American concept of church and state separation, Pope Leo explained that "it would be very erroneous to draw the conclusion that in America is to be sought the type of the most desirable status of the Church, or that it would be universally lawful or expedient for State and Church to be, as in America, dissevered and divorced."[16] In fact, he argued that the American Catholic Church would be better off "if, in addition to liberty, she enjoyed the favor of the laws and the patronage of the public authority."[17] With encouragement from theologians, including the American John Courtney Murray, however, the Church by the 1960s saw the benefits of church and state separation. The Second Vatican Council stated that "the Church, by reason of her role and competence, is not identified with any political community nor bound by ties to any political system. . . . The political community and the Church are autonomous and independent of each other in their own fields."[18] Many were convinced that the Church had suffered from its close alliances with governments in the past. Abuses of the inquisitions and crusades, as well as political corruption in church offices, illustrated that too close an alliance with the political system could distract the Church from her religious mission.[19]

What the Council did not concede, however, was the right of the Church to act as a moral critic of governments and society. According to the Council, "The Church should have true freedom . . . to pass moral judgements even in matters relating to politics, whenever the fundamental rights of man or the salvation of souls requires it."[20] Bishops, the Council argued, "should expound . . . the principles governing the solution of those very grave problems concerning the possession, increase and just distribution of material goods, concerning peace and war, and the fraternal coexistence of all peoples."[21]

The document *Gaudium et spes* (Pastoral Constitution on the Church in the Modern World) issued on December 7, 1965, stands as the most important Council statement addressing church social teaching. Articulating a politically progressive message, the Council encouraged political action and sought to provide a religious basis for political culture. While not intended to be a statement on public policy, the document is strongly suggestive of liberal economic and foreign policies.

An aggressive government role in combating poverty, unemployment, and other economic problems was given strong endorsement. In this respect the Council continued in a tradition going back nearly one hundred years. Church social teaching has long emphasized the public manifestations of faith and the responsibility of citizens and governments. The last century has produced many documents on the social teaching of the Church. Papal encyclicals and pastoral letters as well as Council documents stress the obligation of the temporal world of politics and economics to improve the human condition.

SOCIAL TEACHING, PAPAL ENCYCLICALS, AND THE COUNCIL

In 1991 Catholics celebrated the one hundredth anniversary of *Rerum novarum* (The Condition of Labor), the encyclical by Pope Leo XIII that marks the beginning of the modern social teaching of the Church. *Rerum novarum* is widely recognized as a watershed in modern Catholic social teaching. Pope Pius XI referred to Leo's encyclical as "the Magna Charta upon which all Christian activity in the social field ought to be based."[22]

Pope Leo's encyclical openly confronted liberal capitalism, as he addressed the condition to which "working men have been surrendered, isolated and helpless, to the heartedness of employers and the greed of unchecked competition."[23] While defending the right to private property and asserting that the "main tenet of socialism, community of goods, must be utterly rejected," the pope drew a distinction between the right to ownership and the duty to ensure a just distribution of wealth.[24] Consistent with long-held Catholic teaching, Pope Leo endorsed the use of government as a remedy for social and economic ills, but his principle of just laws required that government intrusion be limited only to that which is essential to alleviate the problem. "The law must not undertake more, nor proceed further, than is required for the remedy of the evil or the removal of the mischief."[25]

But the responsibility of government goes beyond the mere maintenance of law and order. Government has a duty "to make sure that the laws and institutions . . . shall be such as of themselves to realize public well-being and private prosperity."[26] This includes a duty "to promote to the utmost the interests of the poor."[27] This emphasis on the government's obligation to workers and the poor of society marks a break with a past that found the Church closely allied with powerful interests in society. This preferential option for the poor is resounded in later encyclicals, the Second Vatican Council, and the pastoral letters of the American Catholic bishops.

What Leo's encyclical provides in bold principles, however, it lacks in specificity. While Leo endorses efforts by government to remedy social ills, he lays out very general standards. As the pope admits, "We do not judge it possible to enter into minute particulars touching the subject of organization (of government); this must depend on national character, on practice and experience."[28] A major shortcoming of his document is that it offers little guidance on how moral principles can be translated into specific action. Later popes and bishops, however, would build on Leo's teaching and provide more specificity. Citing the ambiguous passages of *Rerum novarum*, Pope Pius XI attempted to answer the doubts raised by Leo's encyclical.

On the occasion of the fortieth anniversary of *Rerum novarum*, Pope Pius XI issued *Quadragesimo anno* (Reconstructing the Social Order), in which he praised the message of Leo and built upon the teaching that government has a responsibility to actively promote justice in society. In conspicuously glowing terms, Pius XI asserts that the encyclical *Rerum novarum* overthrew the "tottering" tenets of liberalism "which had long hampered effective action by the State."[29] He argues that the social policy reforms adopted by many governments to combat economic ills are strongly suggestive of *Rerum novarum*, "to which great credit must be given for whatever improvement has been achieved in the workers' condition."[30] He attributes the rise in confessional labor unions (many organized by the clergy and the Catholic laity) to Leo's call for such unions.[31]

Confronting critics who argue that popes and the church hierarchy are acting out of place by getting involved in matters of politics and economics, Pius reasserts Leo's principle that "there resides in us the right and duty to pronounce with supreme authority upon social and economic matters . . . not of course matters of technique, for which she [the Church] is neither suitably equipped nor endowed by office, but in all things that are concerned with the moral law."[32] In this respect, the Church demands the right to comment on political authority.

According to Pius, "The State and good citizen ought to look to and strive toward this end: that the conflict between the hostile classes be abolished and harmonious cooperation of the Industries and Professions be encouraged and promoted."[33] But the pope did not recognize that capitalism would secure this. Rejecting the tenets of liberal capitalism that free competition can be relied upon to develop and distribute economic wealth justly, Pius argues that "free competition, while justified and certainly useful provided it is kept within certain limits, clearly cannot direct economic life."[34]

As American bishops maintained in their 1986 pastoral letter on the economy, Pope Pius sees government regulation as a solution rather than the cause of economic ills:

Free competition, kept within definite and due limits and still more economic dictatorship, must be effectively brought under public authority in these matters which pertain to the latter's function. The public institutions themselves, of peoples, moreover, ought to make all human society conform to the needs of the common good; that is, to the norm of social justice. If this is done, that most important division of social life, namely, economic activity, cannot fail likewise to return to right and sound order.[35]

This skepticism about capitalism has been echoed in the encyclicals of many popes and found support at the Second Vatican Council.[36] In 1961 Pope John XXIII maintained that changes brought about by societal developments in the twentieth century made government intervention a greater imperative. "The present advance in scientific knowledge and productive technology clearly puts it within the power of the public authority to a much greater degree than ever before to reduce imbalances. . . . Hence the insistent demands on those in authority—since they are responsible for the common good—to increase the degree and scope of their activities in the economic sphere, and to devise ways and means and set the necessary machinery in motion for the attainment of this end."[37] Balancing this with Pope Pius XI's "principle of subsidiarity," however, Pope John stresses that public power "must never be exerted to the extent of depriving the individual citizen of his freedom of action."[38] Communist, socialist, or fascist regimes that deny basic freedoms therefore, cannot justify oppression by arguing that it is done for the public welfare. Any system that denies the preeminent position of the individual and places social institutions before people is in violation of moral law.

How to balance the need for an authority to guide and direct social reform while still maintaining the integrity of free persons is a question the Church confronts with regard to how it governs itself. The Church's rhetoric has not always been matched by its action. One would be hard-pressed to argue that its associations with European fascists during World War II could be reconciled with its calls for freedom and justice. The dilemmas the Church faces today with regard to its treatment of church workers, divorced Catholics, women, and homosexuals are exemplified by current crises. As one anonymous American bishop in our survey put it, "I am not certain that the Church's concern for individual rights and social justice [is] applied adequately to its own members, e.g., women, dissident theologians, [and] its own employees." This concern was shared by many American bishops who, in 1992, voted down the bishops' pastoral letter on women in the Catholic Church.[39]

SOCIAL TEACHING OF VATICAN II

Vatican II can be viewed in the tradition of the major social encyclicals in that it argued for government regulation of the economy and society in order to bring about greater equity. But it also suggested ways to further develop and clarify social teaching by encouraging bishops and episcopal conferences to provide more specificity on that teaching and by supporting a greater role for the laity and experts from outside the Church in the development of pastoral statements.

The Council document *Gaudium et spes* (Pastoral Constitution on the Church in the Modern World) serves as the primary statement on the Church and politics. It is the first such document to address the temporal world, emphasizing the interrelationship between the realms of religion, science, politics, and everyday living. While the Council stresses that "Christ did not bequeath to the Church a mission in the political, economic, or social order," the Church's religious mission "can be the source of commitment, direction, and vigor to establish and consolidate the community of men according to the law of God. In fact, the Church is able, indeed it is obliged, if times and circumstances require it, to initiate action for the benefit of all men, especially of those in need."[40]

This obligation includes the duty of Christians "to work untiringly for fundamental decisions to be taken in economic and political affairs, on the national as well as the international level, which will ensure . . . the dignity of the human person, without distinction of race, sex, nation, religion, or social circumstances."[41] And voting, the Council explains, is not only a citizen's right, but a duty.[42]

While the Church had, since the Reformation, dissuaded Catholic participation with Protestants, Vatican II called for new cooperation. Consistent with its ecumenical spirit, the Council states that it is "desirable, and often imperative, that Catholics cooperate with other Christians, either in activities or in societies . . . at national or international level(s)."[43] The Council fathers hoped that ecumenical associations would encourage "joint enquiry," among Catholics and other Christians, "with a view to taking joint action in and for the world."[44]

Consistent with a general emphasis on the dignity of the person, the Council defines a central role for the individual in political action: "The social nature of man shows that there is an interdependence between personal betterment and the improvement of society. . . . [H]e is and he ought to be the beginning, the subject and the object of every social organization."[45] While many religionists, including fundamentalist Protestants and American bishops of the nineteenth century, stressed the dangers of worldly involvement in politics, according to the Council, "Individual and collective activity . . . presents no problem to believers."[46]

Politics, then, is not something to shy away from, but insofar as it affects the communal well-being, each person has a social responsibility to political action. Stressing the importance of communitarian responsibility, the Council argues that "life in Society is not something accessory to man himself: through his dealings with others, through mutual service, and through fraternal dialogue, man develops all his talents and becomes able to rise to his destiny."[47] It is necessary that "every group must take into account the needs and legitimate aspirations of every other group, and still more of the human family as a whole."[48]

The Catholic teaching dividing Catholics and Protestants since the Reformation, that good works in addition to faith are necessary for salvation, implies a social obligation. According to the Council, this includes political action. "Whoever contributes to the development of the community of mankind on the level of . . . national and international politics, according to God's plan, is also contributing in no small way to the community of the Church."[49] "The best way to fulfil one's obligations of justice and love," the Council states, "is to contribute to the common good . . . even to the point of fostering and helping public and private organizations devoted to bettering the conditions of life."[50] In fact, "the Christian who shirks his temporal duties shirks his duties towards his neighbor, neglects God himself, and endangers his eternal salvation."[51]

As for Catholics "versed" in politics, the Council states, they "should not decline to enter public life."[52] Political education is "vitally necessary" and can be developed through political action: "Those with a talent for the difficult yet noble art of politics . . . should prepare themselves for it, and, forgetting their own convenience and material interests, they should engage in political activity. They must combat injustice and oppression, arbitrary domination and intolerance by individuals or political parties, and they must do so with integrity and wisdom."[53]

Such a call to political action, however, is tempered by an endorsement of political pluralism. Christians "should recognize the legitimacy of differing points of view about the organization of worldly affairs and show respect for their fellow citizens, who even in association defend their opinions by legitimate means," the Council states.[54] The Church would not claim an exclusive truth on questions of politics.

The encouragement of political participation to affect government action stemmed from the Church's recognition that government has a central role in regulating society to ensure justice. "The growing complexity of modern situations makes it necessary for public authority to intervene more often in social, cultural and economic matters in order to bring about more favorable conditions to enable citizens and groups to pursue freely and effectively the achievement of man's well-being in its totality."[55] Governmental power, however, must be restrained and limited by the decisions of the people. The bishops tempered their statement, noting that citizens "should take care not to vest too much power in the hands of public authority nor to make untimely and exaggerated demands for favors and subsidies, lessening in this way the responsible role of individuals, families, and social groups."[56] Democratic responsibilities must be safeguarded to check abusive power.

In keeping with the sentiments of earlier popes, the Council warned against the tendency for economic thinking to become dominant over other values. "The ultimate and basic purpose of economic production does not consist merely in the increase of goods produced, nor in profit nor in prestige; it is directed to the service of man, that is in his totality, taking into account his material needs and the requirements of his intellectual, moral, spiritual, and religious life; of all men whomsoever and of every group of men of whatever race or from whatever part of the world."[57] In order "to fulfill the requirements of justice and equity, every effort must be made to put an end as soon as possible to the immense economic inequalities which exist in the world."[58] The use of government as a tool to remedy inequalities, solidly backed by popes and bishops since Leo XIII, was heartily endorsed by Vatican II. Unrestrained capitalism cannot assure economic equity. While the Church historically has upheld the right to private property, the Council states that "the state has the duty to prevent anyone from abusing his private property to the detriment of the common good."[59]

Providing a wider decision-making authority could help secure greater equity from economic activity. Just as the Church endorsed collaborative inquiry with experts in science and religion, both inside and outside the Church, it also called for collective decision making in the economic realm. Because of the wide impact of economic decisions, the Council states that decisions "of general interest" must be made by the widest group possible.[60] In private business, the Council called for greater participation among workers in the decisions that will affect them. "Taking into account the role of every person concerned—owners, employers, management, and employees—and without weakening the necessary executive unity, the active participation of everybody in administration is to be encouraged."[61] Similar calls would be made by American Catholic bishops in their 1984 pastoral letter on the economy.

The Council left the development of more specific applications of these principles to bishops and the laity within each country. Rome could not be expected to provide one teaching applicable to every cultural context. Therefore, church leaders within each nation were asked to assume a more active teaching responsibility on questions of politics and economics.

Bolstered by the Council, American bishops have sought through pastoral letters, public statements, and individual sermons to encourage American Catholics to apply their religious faith in the advancement of political and social objectives. This has been done, however, with extensive consultation and dialogue with the laity and experts in government, science, and religion.

ELEVATED ROLE OF BISHOPS AND LAITY IN THE CHURCH

While Vatican I emphasized the preeminent position of the pope through its declaration of papal primacy and infallibility, Vatican II has been called the "bishops' council." By emphasizing the collegial teaching authority of Catholic bishops in union with the pope, their position within the Church received a big boost.

As "representatives" of Christ, the Council states, bishops are teachers, shepherds, and priests.[62] They are "teachers endowed with the authority of Christ, who preach the faith to the people assigned to them, the faith which is destined to inform their thinking and direct their conduct."[63]

Seeking to link religious faith to temporal action, the Council called upon bishops to inform Catholics on church social teaching. The Council encouraged bishops to use public statements, the press, and other media to illuminate the Church's teaching on morality related to issues of public policy.[64] Conferences of bishops and national conferences were touted as effective vehicles to achieve these goals.[65]

The American bishops' response has been quick and vigorous. Since the National Conference of Catholic Bishops was established in 1967, the bishops have issued more than 150 statements on public issues. In contrast to the papal encyclicals and Council documents issued prior to Vatican II, the statements of American bishops have differed in at least two important ways. First, American bishops offer more specificity on how moral principles can be translated into public policy positions. In their 1987 pastoral on economics, the American bishops justify their recommendations for specific economic policy reforms, stating that, "We feel obligated to teach by example how Christians can undertake concrete analysis and make specific judgments on economic issues. The church's teachings cannot be left at the level of appealing generalities."[66] This departure from "appealing generalities" left the bishops vulnerable to critics who contend that bishops have neither the expertise nor the authority to endorse specific policies. Leaving the safer domain of generality makes the bishops' activities more controversial.

Second, the American bishops differ from their pre–Vatican II predecessors in that they have attempted to bring lay Catholics and outside experts into their deliberations on major pastoral letters. This precedent was set at the Vatican Council itself, where lay Catholics and non-Catholics alike were allowed to participate. The Council encouraged bishops to seek help from the laity and to utilize social research.[67] In writing their pastoral letters on peace and the economy, the American bishops have relied extensively on assistance from the laity. With the help of the United States Catholic Conference (USCC) staff and numerous public hearings, they have researched the issues of social concern upon which they speak.

As for the laity, the Council states that they "are called to participate actively in the whole life of the Church."[68] The Church recognized that the laity had much to offer: "By reason of the knowledge, competence or pre-eminence which they have, the laity are empowered—indeed sometimes obliged—to manifest their opinion on those things which pertain to the good of the Church."[69] In an uncommon show of modesty, Council fathers acknowledged the value of lay contributions.

CONCLUSION

In many respects the extraordinary Second Vatican Council fundamentally altered the Roman Catholic Church and its approach to politics. Current debate within the Church over questions of free inquiry for theologians and calls for more democracy within the Church can only be understood in light of the promises of Vatican II. The ascendance of American Catholic bishops from timid leaders of a minority religion in American society to a position as major religious-political spokesmen must be viewed in the context of Vatican II changes. The politics of American Catholic bishops is the topic of the next chapter.

NOTES

1. See Eugene C. Bianchi, "John XXIII, Vatican II, and American Catholicism," *Annals of the American Academy of Political and Social Science* 387 (January 1970), pp. 30–40.

2. Quoted in Anne Lally Milhaven, "Dissent Within the U.S. Church: An Interview with Charles Curran," in Mary C. Segers, ed., *Church Polity and American Politics: Issues in Contemporary American Catholicism* (New York: Garland, 1990), p. 288.

3. Cardinal Joseph Bernardin points out that while the Council call was a surprise in many respects, "the Council was in continuity with the past." He argues that some developments in biblical, liturgical, and catechetical reforms were partially underway during the reign of Pope Pius XII. See Alberic Stacpoole, ed., *Vatican II Revisited by Those who Were There* (London: Geoffrey Chapman, 1986), p. xii.

4. Robert McAfee Brown, *Observer in Rome: A Protestant Report on the Vatican Council* (Garden City, N.Y.: Doubleday, 1964), pp. 6–7.

5. Quoted in Henri Daniel-Rops, *The Second Vatican Council: The Story Behind the Ecumenical Council of Pope John XXIII* (New York: Hawthorn Books, 1962), p. 13.

6. Such councils are relatively rare in Church history, although the exact number (21 or 22) is disputable, given the questionable standing of some popes (or antipopes). See Daniel-Rops, *The Second Vatican Council*, pp. 25–32.

7. Quoted in Loris F. Capovilla, "Reflections on the Twentieth Anniversary," in Stacpoole, *Vatican II Revisited*, p. 122.

8. The argument for a reconciliation between religion and science is forcefully made by Teilhard de Chardin in *The Phenomenon of Man* (New York: Harper, 1959).

9. Quoted in Capovilla, "Reflections," pp. 122–123.

10. Quoted in Yves Congar, "Moving Towards a Pilgrim Church," in Stacpoole, *Vatican II Revisited*, pp. 142–143.

11. Boniface VIII, *Unam sanctam*, 1302, quoted in R. Freeman Butts, *The American Tradition in Religion and Education* (Boston: Beacon Press, 1950), p. 13.

12. Quoted in Congar, "Moving Towards a Pilgrim Church," p. 133.

13. Quoted in ibid., p. 139.

14. Leo XIII, *Immortale dei* in Claudia Carlen, *The Papal Encyclicals*, vol. 2 (Wilmington, N.C.: McGrath, 1981) p. 108, par. 3.

15. Ibid., par. 6.

16. Leo XIII, *Longinqua*, in Carlen, *Encyclicals*, vol. 2, pp. 364–365, par. 6.

17. Ibid.

18. Vatican Council II, *Gaudium et spes*, December 7, 1965, in Austin P. Flannery, ed., *Documents of Vatican II* (Grand Rapids, Mich.: Eerdmans, 1975), p. 984, par. 76.

19. See Rodger Charles and Drostan Maclaren, *The Social Teaching of Vatican II* (San Francisco: Ignatius Press, 1982), pp. 38–48.

20. Vatican Council II, *Gaudium et spes*, in Flannery, *Documents*, p. 985, par. 76.

21. Vatican Council II, *Christus dominus*, October 28, 1965, in Flannery, *Documents*, p. 570, par. 12.

22. Pius XI, *Quadragesimo anno*, May 15, 1931, in Carlen, *Encyclicals*, vol. 3, p. 420, par. 39.

23. Leo XIII, *Rerum novarum*, May 15, 1891, in Carlen, *Encyclicals*, vol. 2, p. 242, par. 3.

24. Ibid., p. 244, par. 15.

25. Ibid., p. 251, par. 36.

26. Ibid., p. 249, par. 32.

27. Ibid.

28. Ibid., p. 255, par. 56.

29. Pius XI, *Quadragesimo anno*, in Carlen, *Encyclicals*, vol. 3, p. 419, par. 27.

30. Ibid., par. 28.

31. In no uncertain terms Pope Leo gave his blessing to organized labor: "We may lay it down as a general and lasting law that working men's associations should be so organized and governed as to furnish the best and most suitable means for attaining what is aimed at, that is to say, for helping each individual member to better his condition to the utmost in body, soul and property" (Leo XIII, *Rerum novarum*, in Carlen, *Encyclicals*, vol. 2, p. 255, par. 57).

32. Pius XI, *Quadragesimo anno*, in Carlen, *Encyclicals*, vol. 3, p. 421, par. 41.

33. Ibid., p. 428, par. 81.

34. Ibid., p. 429, par. 88.

35. Ibid., p. 432, par. 110.

36. See Michael Novak, *The Spirit of Democratic Capitalism* (New York: Simon and Schuster, 1982).

37. John XXIII, *Mater et magistra*, May 15, 1961, in Carlen, *Encyclicals*, vol. 5, p. 65, par. 54.

38. Ibid., par. 55.

39. See "Yes, We Can, No, You Can't: Why Women's Pastoral Was Defeated," in *National Catholic Reporter,* December 4, 1992, pp. 2–5.

40. Vatican Council II, *Gaudium et spes*, in Flannery, *Documents*, p. 942, par. 42.

41. Ibid., p. 964, par. 60.

42. Ibid., p. 982, par. 75.

43. Vatican Council II, *Apostolican actuositatem*, November 18, 1965, in Flannery, *Documents*, p. 792, par. 27.

44. Secretariat for the Promotion of the Unity of Christians, "Reflections and Suggestions Concerning Ecumenical Dialogue," August 15, 1970, in Flannery, *Documents*, p. 551, chap. 7, par. 4.

45. Vatican Council II, *Gaudium et spes*, in Flannery, *Documents*, p. 926, par. 25.

46. Ibid., p. 933, par. 34.

47. Ibid., p. 926, par. 25.

48. Ibid., p. 927, par. 26.

49. Ibid., p. 947, par. 44.

50. Ibid., p. 930, par. 30.

51. Ibid., p. 943, par. 43.

52. Vatican Council II, *Apostolican actuositatem*, in Flannery, *Documents*, p. 782, par. 14.

53. Vatican Council II, *Gaudium et spes*, in Flannery, *Documents*, p. 984, par. 75.

54. Ibid., p. 983, par. 75.

55. Ibid.

56. Ibid., pp. 982–983, par. 75.

57. Ibid., p. 970, par. 64.

58. Ibid., p. 971, par. 66.

59. Ibid., p. 978, par. 71.

60. Ibid., p. 971, par. 65.

61. Ibid., p. 974, par. 68.

62. Vatican Council II, *Lumen gentium*, November 21, 1964, in Flannery, *Documents*, p. 374, par. 21.

63. Ibid., p. 379, par. 25.

64. Vatican Council II, *Christus dominus*, October 28, 1965, in Flannery, *Documents*, p. 571, par. 13.

65. Ibid., p. 574, par. 18.

66. National Conference of Catholic Bishops, "Economic Justice for All: Catholic Social Teaching and the U.S. Economy," in Hugh J. Nolan, ed., *Pastoral Letters of the United States Catholic Bishops*, vol. 5, 1983–1988 (Washington, D.C.: United States Catholic Conference, 1989), p. 375.

67. Vatican Council II, *Christus dominus*, in Flannery, *Documents*, p. 573, par. 16.

68. Vatican Council II, *Gaudium et spes*, in Flannery, *Documents*, p. 944, par. 43.

69. Vatican Council II, *Lumen gentium*, in Flannery, *Documents*, p. 394, par. 37.

Chapter 5 _____

Politics and the U.S. Catholic Bishops

With encouragement from the Second Vatican Council, and bolstered by the election of John F. Kennedy as America's first Catholic president, American Catholic bishops have become increasingly active politically. Through the National Conference of Catholic Bishops (NCCB), American prelates have taken positions on a variety of public policy issues as they have sought to influence political debate. With their highly publicized pastoral letters, "The Challenge of Peace" and "Economic Justice for All," Catholic bishops reached center stage as political-religious leaders.[1] But critics of the bishops' conference, pressure from the Vatican, and division within the hierarchy itself cast a cloud of uncertainty over the future direction of the bishops' political involvement.

Activities at the NCCB are under attack from many fronts. The bishops' policy recommendations are questioned and their political expertise is challenged.[2] Francis Winters discounts the bishops' contribution to the nuclear weapons debate, asserting that "all the critics regard the teaching of the pastoral letter, which condemns all militarily meaningful use of the nuclear arsenal, as an anachronistic exercise in the nuclear age."[3] Dinesh D'Souza claims that "interviews with . . . bishops suggest that they know little or nothing about the ideas and proposals to which they are putting their signature and lending their religious authority."[4] Though endorsed by the Second Vatican Council, theologians debate the degree to which national conferences of bishops carry teaching authority.[5] And critics in Rome have expressed concern over the Americans' actions.[6]

The NCCB is at a crossroads with regard to its place in public political debate. Even among themselves there are bishops questioning whether the NCCB can retain a position of leadership. The head of the bishops' committee that drafted the pastoral letter on the economy, Archbishop Rembert Weakland of Milwaukee, sees the role of the bishops' conference declining if the Church emphasizes its authoritarian positions on controversial issues like abortion and the ordination of women. According to Weakland, "It will be difficult to maintain the present style of authority in a world that is everywhere . . . looking for more participatory structures. . . . As I see things evolving, the conference of bishops is going to become less and less important. . . . Maybe bishops will cease to hold the kind of leadership we had in the past decade."[7] Former NCCB president Archbishop Daniel Pilarczyk of Cincinnati describes a similar shift, though he emphasizes a different cause: "It may be that we're going to have to deal with some of these internal questions on a more urgent basis in the next couple of years, and, given the fact that you can only do so much, the big splashy social questions may not be our main event."[8]

Will the bishops push forward with the Second Vatican Council's call to actively engage in the political debate on economic and defense-related issues, or will we see a triumph of traditionalists who prefer that the church emphasize other issues and focus its attention on spiritual and church-related issues? As the NCCB prioritizes abortion as the most important issue of public policy, will the progressive wing of the hierarchy be silenced? These questions are difficult to answer without a better understanding of the individuals that comprise the membership of the NCCB, the American bishops themselves. Though bishops are often referred to as if they are a solid bloc, important political differences exist among them. Current changes underway in the NCCB can be attributed to the struggle between competing visions of the Church's social mission.

General conclusions concerning the attitudes of bishops can be drawn from pastoral letters and council documents, but many bishops have minimal, if any, influence in the development of these statements. Content analysis of the bishops' collective statements offers only a partial picture. This chapter utilizes the results of our survey of the American bishops to gain a better understanding of the political attitudes of this elite group of religious leaders.

HISTORICAL BACKGROUND

American Catholic bishops have come a long way from their nine-teenth-century warnings that Catholics should avoid the dangers of political strife and controversy. The bishops' 1979 pastoral statement, "Political Responsibility: Choices for the 1980s," which encourages the faithful to engage in the political process and "to become involved in the campaign or party of your choice," marks a significant change in attitude.[9]

For many years Catholic prelates in the United States hesitated to become politically involved or to give instruction on politics. With the exception of a few prominent church spokesmen such as John Carroll, John Ireland, James Gibbons, and Francis Spellman, most Catholic clerics shied away from politics. The predominant view among Catholic clergy was that their work was primarily religious. As John Tracy Ellis puts it, "The policy of clerical aloofness from politics was in part induced by the shyness of an unpopular minority, but it was equally a policy born of the dual conviction that the clergy's principal business was their religious ministry and that it was improper to use their office for political ends."[10] The bishops' Fourth Provincial Council in May 1840 ended with a pastoral letter indicating the bishops' reticence. To American Catholics, they said, "We disclaim all right to interfere with your judgment in the political affairs of our common country, and are far from entertaining the wish to control you in the constitutional exercise of your freedom."[11] However, warning against the dangers of political controversy, the bishops told Catholics to "avoid the contaminating influence of political strife, keep yourself aloof from the pestilential atmosphere in which honor, virtue, patriotism and religion perish."[12] Criticism of government policy was discouraged. Catholics seeking to demonstrate their loyalty and patriotism became among the staunchest defenders of the government.

The bishops' reluctance to involve themselves actively in political controversy can be attributed to several factors. As members of a persecuted ethnic minority in many parts of the United States, Catholics feared engaging in political conflict. As Thomas McAvoy points out, "The lack of numbers gave the Catholics of that day little inclination to bring their religion into politics."[13] Attempts to use their religion to justify political action might have led to intensified nativist sentiment.

The bishops' aloofness from politics exemplified the manifestations of a "ghetto mentality" that many Catholics shared.[14] Lack of interest in intellectual and scholarly pursuits and a desire to keep in one's social place kept many Catholics from venturing beyond their ethnoreligious community. Benefits derived from isolation offered strong incentives to maintain ethnic ties. Remnants of strong cultural and ethnic affinities that set American Catholics apart from their Protestant neighbors still endure.[15] James Penning's findings suggest that the effects of group integration characterized by the ethnic neighborhood provide a better predictor of Catholics' political behavior than group identification alone.[16]

While the turn of the century brought political activism among Protestant clerics inspired by the Social Gospel Movement, few prominent Catholics took part. Instead, Catholics were preoccupied with building up private charitable institutions and charity groups such as the Society of St. Vincent de Paul.[17] The lack of political activism did not signify a lack in social concern. For Catholics, the parish and local community provided an arena for social action.[18]

World War I marked a turning point for the American bishops. In order to coordinate Catholic efforts during the war, the bishops formed the National Catholic War Council in 1917.[19] This council served to unite American Catholics behind the war effort. After the war many bishops recognized potential political benefits that might be realized by retaining some form of the national organization. As Bishop Peter J. Muldoon of Rockford, Illinois stated, "We do not hesitate to say that some representative body could accomplish untold good. . . . There is an incessant demand for instruction on 'how to act' on many bills that are now before the legislatures of the country."[20]

Not all bishops agreed, however, that such an organization was a good idea. Some members of the hierarchy questioned the wisdom of bishops becoming politically active in this way. Others were concerned that a national conference might infringe upon the domain of authority of individual bishops in their dioceses.[21]

Despite the concern, the bishops decided to set up a national organization through which they could develop a social policy platform. In 1919 they created the National Catholic Welfare Council (NCWC). After some prodding, a reluctant Vatican gave its approval to the new organization. There was concern that the canon law term "council" might lead some to conclude that the actions of the organization carried the same weight as conciliar legislation, so at the request of the Consistorial Congregation of the Holy See the name was changed to the National Catholic Welfare Conference.

In February 1919 the pamphlet *Social Reconstruction: A General Review of the Problems and Surveys of Remedies,* written by Monsignor John A. Ryan, was given official endorsement by the bishops of the Administrative Committee of the NCWC. This statement, later formalized as a pastoral letter, offered suggestions on a variety of social programs, including endorsements of a minimum wage, health and unemployment insurance, and the right of workers to organize in unions.[22] Among the more controversial (and prophetic) policy recommendations, the bishops declared that "the state should make comprehensive provision for insurance against illness, invalidity, unemployment, and old age."[23] This document put the bishops in the forefront among those endorsing relatively radical policies for that time, and it opened them to stern criticism.

National Association of Manufacturers (NAM) president Stephen C. Mason criticized the bishops, stating that "it is our belief that a careful reading of this pamphlet will lead you to the conclusion . . . that it involves what may prove to be a covert effort to disseminate partisan, pro-labor, socialistic propaganda under the official insignia of the Roman Catholic Church in America."[24] Nearly a decade later, a report of the Joint Legislative Committee Investigating Seditious Activities of New York State identified the bishops' statement as the work of "a certain group in the Catholic Church with leanings toward Socialism."[25] Even within the hierarchy some worried. Cardinal O'Connell once referred to Monsignor Ryan as "a Bolshevik in a red cassock."[26]

It is difficult to determine how much influence the bishops' pastoral statement had in affecting public policy or the views of their followers. While eleven of the twelve proposals included therein were eventually enacted into law, proponents for these changes came from a variety of circles. Also questionable is the Church's influence on Catholic politicians. Even among high-ranking Catholics in government, knowledge of Catholic social teaching was not extensive. When the 1928 Democratic presidential candidate, Catholic Governor of New York Al Smith, was challenged in an open letter to the *Atlantic Monthly* on papal claims on church and state relations, Smith replied, "So little are these matters of the essence of my faith that I, a devout Catholic since childhood, never heard of them until I read your letter."[27]

The civil rights struggles of the 1950s and 1960s sparked another round of activism. The bishops condemned racial segregation in their 1958 pastoral statement, "Discrimination and Christian Conscience."[28] Individual bishops took actions against public figures to emphasize this position. Speaking out against segregationist politicians, Bishop Paul J. Hallinan of Charleston, South Carolina, warned that "the devout Catholic cannot support segregation in any way." This, he went on, "applies to any political candidate with that stand."[29] New Orleans Archbishop Joseph Francis Rummel went so far as to excommunicate segregationist leader Leander Perez for his white supremacist views, and Archbishop Oscar Lipscomb (then of New Orleans) used excommunication to sanction members of the Ku Klux Klan. Many· Southern bishops, however, spoke out against segregation only after national trends were moving in that direction.

Catholicism was still very much a minority religion in the South, and bishops' hesitancy lingered longer there.[30]

With the coming of the Second Vatican Council, bishops greatly increased their political involvement. The Council marked a major turning point in Catholic history and in the political aggressiveness of the American Church. Vatican II did not start the process of social activism, but it greatly accelerated it. Its emphasis on episcopal collegiality gave bishops new encouragement to speak out and participate in the political process. Whereas Vatican I convened in 1869 to reassert the pope's authority in the face of secular and religious attacks, Vatican II stressed the power of bishops. The Vatican II emphasis on the bishops' collegial authority gave a boost to bishops just as the Vatican I decree on the doctrine of papal infallibility reinforced the position of the pope. Bolstered by support from the Council, American bishops accepted a greater leadership role.[31]

The Council stressed a need for bishops to offer political guidance. As stated in conciliar documents, bishops "should expound . . . the principles governing the solution of those very grave problems concerning the possession, increase and just distribution of material goods, concerning peace and war, and the fraternal coexistence of all peoples."[32] Bishops were encouraged to make statements on public policy and to use the press and other media for this purpose. Conferences of bishops and national conferences were touted as effective vehicles to achieve these goals.[33]

Bishops in the United States answered the Council's call by establishing the National Conference of Catholic Bishops in 1966. The increase in the number of politically related pastoral letters since the Council signified a willingness on the part of the hierarchy to play a greater role in the political debate.

The bishops were also given encouragement from the improved social position Catholics had achieved by the 1960s. The achievement of economic and educational parity with Protestants helped to move Catholics into the mainstream of American life. Gains in educational achievement and post–World War II acculturation of ethnics erased the socioeconomic advantages Protestants once held over Catholics.[34] The American Catholic Church was no longer an immigrant church. Since Catholicism was a persecuted ethnic minority in nineteenth-century America, Catholic reluctance to engage in the controversy of politics might be understood in terms of self-preservation. By the mid-twentieth century, however, American Catholics had "arrived." With the election of John Kennedy as America's first Catholic president in 1960, anti-Catholic fears subsided. Political hopefuls no longer needed to fear that their religion would be a stumbling block to higher political office. And the United States Catholic bishops entered a new era.

The NCCB saw its effort come alive through unprecedented activism in the 1980s. Months of consultation with experts in government, business, education, and religion yielded the most comprehensive, highly researched documents ever offered by the American hierarchy. The bishops commanded not only national, but world attention with the issuance of "Challenge of Peace" and "Economic Justice for All."

Rejecting the belief that the use of nuclear weapons could ever be morally justified, the bishops called for an end to the arms race and deep cuts in defense spending. Risking the label of socialism, they sharply criticized the shortcomings of American capitalism. The bishops pushed for increased government efforts to ensure economic security for all persons and endorsed a system to secure greater worker participation in business decisions.

Then the focus shifted. In November 1989 the bishops decided to make abortion a top priority.[35] After the Supreme Court, in *Webster v. Reproductive Health Services* (1989), expressed a willingness to allow certain state restrictions on abortions, the issue resurfaced in the political debate.[36] And bishops took up the pro-life cause with vigor.

Now in the 1990s, emphasis on economic and foreign policy issues is lessening. The voices of the progressive wing of the hierarchy that were vocal during the 1980s are intermittent. The American hierarchy is becoming less vocal on issues that comprise the "liberal agenda" evident in their pastoral letters on peace and the economy and is devoting increased attention to the abortion issue.

This shift has potentially wide repercussions. Most leaders agree that the Church has the authority to speak on economic and foreign policy issues, but more conservative clerics argue that while disagreement with the bishops on these issues is permissible, the same is not true for abortion. Vatican II emphasized a need for dialogue between the laity and clergy, but church policy on abortion, according to Rome, is not open for discussion. Archbishop Rembert Weakland of Milwaukee is one of a very few bishops willing to speak publicly on the side of dialogue on the abortion issue as well, but Weakland puts himself at risk of retribution from Rome.[37]

This move toward a more authoritarian posture has coincided with the ascendance of more conservative bishops to leadership positions. Richard McBrien suggests that the current pope is attempting to curtail the liberal wing of the American hierarchy and slow down the reforms of Vatican II.[38] Through the appointment of theologically conservative bishops, rigidly allegiant to the pope, John Paul II is attempting to rein in the American hierarchy.[39]

Action on the new church catechism exemplifies the new Vatican style. Leaving little time for discussion, Rome asked for quick approval from the American bishops. Some bishops worried, however, that American influence would be thwarted as the Vatican limited time for consultation. As Bishop Raymond Lucker of New Ulm, Minnesota, put it, "One of the most important contributions that American bishops can make toward the development of the universal catechism is to share with the universal church our experience with consultation. . . . The most important thing I want to say to the writing committee is: Slow down. Consult with the people." As Lucker sees it, the universal catechism endorsed by Rome "does to some extent go back to [pre-Vatican II] expressions."[40]

In recent episcopal appointments, more conservative clerics, strongly committed to official church doctrine on birth control, ordination of women, and priest celibacy, are given priority. This increase in the number of theologically conservative bishops affects the political outlook of the NCCB. A declining emphasis on economic and defense issues and greater resources committed to the anti-abortion cause signal a shift. But does this imply long-term change? Will recent papal appointments yield significant change in the nature of NCCB political involvement? To answer these questions a better understanding of the political makeup of the Catholic hierarchy in America is needed.

Despite the high public profile of the American Catholic hierarchy, little is known about bishops as individuals, particularly their political views. Studies analyzing NCCB pastoral letters and the pronouncements of individual bishops offer some insight,[41] but not enough is known about how opinions vary within the hierarchy on political issues. As Eugene Kennedy and Victor J. Heckler note, "Empirical research by psychologists and sociologists on bishops . . . is apparently non-existent."[42] Until now, no comprehensive political survey of the United States Catholic bishops has been conducted.

Researchers studying elites are limited by access barriers.[43] Securing the participation of enough bishops is difficult. When in 1966 the *National Catholic Reporter*, a prominent weekly newspaper, sent questionnaires to 225 bishops asking for comments on the Vietnam War, only six bishops replied.[44]

Insight into the political views of bishops has come through studies that focus on a small number of bishops. In interviews with twenty-two Catholic Church leaders (including some bishops), Mary Hanna found this elite to be liberal politically.[45] But the small sample size makes generalizations problematic. Thomas Reese interviewed archbishops in the United States on a range of Church-related issues.[46] His project is a great achievement in that he was able to convince all thirty-one archbishops to participate in his study. Although he discusses tensions within the NCCB over the organization's political direction, the politics of the bishops is not his central focus. Illustrating a need to study the individual political views of bishops, Reese quotes Archbishop Whealon of Hartford saying, "One of the secrets of the Catholic church is how independent the bishop is."[47] Not all bishops agree with the policy positions taken in NCCB pastoral statements. And differences of opinion exist over the proper political role for the bishops.

In a separate study, Reese surveyed all U.S. bishops to ascertain information on the bishops' social and educational background.[48] The tremendous response rate (90 percent) may be attributed to the narrow focus of the questionnaire, which did not address political issues.

In an extensive study of Catholic priests sanctioned by the NCCB, Andrew Greeley also surveyed the bishops on positions concerning a wide variety of church-related concerns and a few political issues.[49] He found the bishops to be more liberal than priests on the issue of a guaranteed annual income. Greeley's study, however, did not concentrate on the political attitudes of the clergy, and he asked very few questions directly related to the bishops' political views.

From a survey of Christian religious elites across several denominations, Lerner, Rothman, and Lichter found evidence to support the conventional wisdom that Catholic leaders are liberal on economics and foreign affairs and conservative on social issues.[50] While this study did not focus on Catholic bishops, the authors included in their sample individuals in positions of leadership from the National Conference of Catholic Bishops.

Still lacking are data that would help us explain differences of opinion among the American bishops and clearer measures to determine the extent to which this religious elite is similar politically to its followers.

Opinion differences within the hierarchy may help explain recent policy shifts at the NCCB. In the 1990s, emphasis on economic and foreign policy issues is lessening. The voices of the progressive wing of the hierarchy that were vocal during the 1980s are intermittent. The American hierarchy is becoming less vocal on issues that comprise the liberal agenda evident in their pastoral letters on peace and the economy and is devoting increased attention to the abortion issue.

The present study utilizes the results of a survey of the American bishops to gain a better understanding of the political attitudes of this elite group of religious leaders and the factors contributing to opinion differences within the American Catholic hierarchy.

THE SAMPLE

There are approximately 380 active and retired bishops in the United States. All active archbishops, bishops, and auxiliary bishops are members of the NCCB. On most issues, all members have equal voting privileges. But only bishops that head dioceses are permitted to vote on financial issues. While retired bishops do not have a vote in the NCCB, they are welcome to participate in policy discussions.

To investigate the personal politics of the bishops, we solicited their views on a variety of issues. The findings from this study are derived from survey responses received from United States Catholic bishops between 1989 and 1990. An initial mailing of a 95-item questionnaire was undertaken. Those not responding to the initial request were sent a second questionnaire six weeks later. One hundred and fifty bishops—or approximately 40 percent—returned usable questionnaires. Responses were received from all regions of the country and from all ranks. Response rates by region of country were as follows: Pacific and Mountain, 40 percent; West Central, 35 percent; East Central, 40 percent; Atlantic, 47 percent; New England, 39 percent; South, 33 percent. Thirty-one percent of the sample consists of bishops appointed by Pope John Paul II. Fifty-two percent were appointed by Pope Paul VI, and 25 percent were appointed by Pope John XXIII or earlier popes. Forty percent of the sample includes bishops under the age of sixty. Thirty-eight percent are between sixty and seventy. Twenty-two percent are over seventy. Nine percent of the sample are archbishops, 50 percent are bishops, 27 percent are auxiliary bishops, and 15 percent of the sample are retired bishops. (Total does not equal 100 percent due to rounding.)

The survey instrument included closed-ended questions on public policy issues, the bishops' political activities, and general attitudes about the role of the Church in politics. The bishops were also invited to submit additional written comments, and over one-third of the respondents offered elaborations on their views. The bishops were assured that their identities would be kept confidential. Quotes that are not footnoted are taken from questionnaire responses.

SOCIAL BACKGROUND

American bishops enjoy the gains in social mobility that have been achieved by many Catholics over the last several decades. While most bishops come from blue-collar families, they well surpass the educational levels of their parents. Twenty-six percent of the bishops claim at least one

Table 5.1
Bishops' Self-Described Nationalities (Percentages)

Irish	55%	French	6%
German	15	Polish	5
Hispanic	7	Black	4
Italian	7	Scandinavian	1

n = 145

parent who graduated from college. But for nearly 50 percent of the bishops, neither of their parents graduated from high school.

Consistent with the results of Reese's survey, we found the American bishops to be very well educated.[51] Seventy-seven percent of the respondents hold graduate degrees, primarily in fields of religious study. For many of these men who came from poor families, free seminary and graduate education provided by the Church offered opportunities their families otherwise could not afford.

In the early years of the American Church, foreign bishops and priests were brought to the United States to alleviate the domestic shortage of qualified clerics. But the American Church is no longer dominated by foreign-born bishops. Ninety-five percent of survey respondents were born in the United States.

Remnants of heavy Irish Catholic immigration to the United States remain, as shown in Table 5.1. Fifty-five percent of the bishops claim an Irish heritage. While Irish is the predominant background of national origin of the American hierarchy, the Church is making partial inroads in diversifying its leaders. Within the past few years, an increasing number of black and Hispanic bishops have been appointed in the United States.

VATICAN II AND POLITICAL ACTIVISM

As an indication of the institutional success of the Catholic Church, nearly all of the bishops surveyed speak positively of Vatican II and the Church's social teaching.[52] A typical comment is offered by one bishop who says, "Vatican II documents contain an enormous wealth of material for teaching people the importance of social issues. The Church Fathers presented an excellent exposition of [the] Church's responsibility on the part of all members towards acquiring a social consciousness." Some bishops, however, are not satisfied with the progress of the Church since the Council, particularly concerning the implementation of the political and social teachings of the Council. While only 1 percent of the bishops believe that the Church has "gone too far" in implementing the social and political teachings of Vatican II, better than one-third (34 percent) feel that she has not gone far enough in these areas. As one of the latter group flatly states, "Too little is being done in Rome and in the U.S. to implement Vatican II." Another bishop, elaborating on why he believes the Church has not gone far enough, explains, "I am not certain that the Church's concern for individual rights and social justice [is] applied adequately to its own members, e.g., women, dissident theologians, its own employees."

In general, the bishops are supportive of their pastorals and the increased public activism of the American hierarchy. "[I] firmly believe [the] Church must make contributions of moral leadership in shaping U.S. domestic and foreign policy," says one bishop. "U.S. Bishops have a right and a duty to teach through pastoral letters in order to instruct Catholics concerning their duties as citizens of a country and as Catholics," says another. Expressing an almost militant fervor, another declares, "The U.S. Bishops must be players in the realm of politics in so far as they concern the Gospel values we claim to espouse even at the risk of penalties from the government."

Some would prefer that the bishops go even further in speaking out. As one bishop puts it, "Catholic bishops should speak to their own constituencies and Catholic politicians—reminding them of the Church's social teachings. There has been too much equivocation by the American bishops. . . . We need more leadership and less public image." Another blames the bishops themselves for the fact that their pastorals did not have as wide an impact as they had hoped. "The U.S. Bishops' [NCCB] dismal failure to implement its major pastorals in the church itself has undermined their documents' practical credibility."

In contrast, there are those who are concerned that some restraint may be in order. "Our bishops should not be speaking out on every political issue," warns one bishop, "but only on those which are high priority and which more directly involve morality (abortion, racism, family life, crime, violence, Catholic schools)."

Many stress that the bishops should remain strictly nonpartisan. Canon law prevents clerics from holding public office, but other forms of clerical involvement in politics is a topic of controversy for the Church.[53] Some bishops are troubled by the use of the word "politics" when referring to their activities. Many seem to view the word as a pejorative term. They are sensitive to charges levied by those who say the bishops are too "political."[54] As one bishop puts it, "The U.S. Bishops do not engage in partisan or political activities. . . . Teaching and working for social justice as taught by scriptures is not political action, it is teaching God's word." While the distinction may be a fine one, it is one that many bishops stress.

There are worries among the hierarchy that the Church will be hurt by signs of division. One bishop expressed reservations about being a participant in the present study: "I was very uncomfortable with this questionnaire.... I fear your publication will not promote Christian integrated social responsibility."

The bishops do not appear to be excessively optimistic about their influence over Catholics' political thinking. As one bishop puts it, "The vast majority of Catholics in the U.S. have at best an impoverished understanding of the role of the contemporary social teaching of the Church in their own lives." Another offers a similar assessment: "In my estimation the documents on peace and economics have been largely ignored by the ordinary Catholic—except those with a pacifist bent." Alluding to American attitudes toward authority, another writes, "I am happy that we bishops have taught and written, as a body and in our dioceses, from the principles of Vatican II. But I'm not convinced of our hearing from the public, both Catholic and non. I am convinced that many, many Catholics—like many Protestants—are more American than Catholic (Protestant)."

POLITICAL PARTICIPATION

The Second Vatican Council encouraged increased political activism on the part of the laity and the bishops. According to the Council, "Whoever contributes to the development of the community of mankind on the level of ... national and international politics, according to God's plan, is also contributing in no small way to the community of the Church."[55]

This includes a Christian duty "to work untiringly for fundamental decisions to be taken in economic and political affairs, on the national as well as the international level, which will ensure ... the dignity of the human person, without distinction of race, sex, nation, religion, or social circumstances."[56] Voting, the Council explains, is not only a political right, but an obligation.[57]

American bishops echo the Council's words in their statement, "Political Responsibility: Choices for the 1980s," and individual bishops are responding personally to the message.[58] Sixty percent of this study's respondents say they give sermons on politics, as Table 5.2 indicates. Twenty-five percent report giving money to a candidate, party, or political action committee. A full 42 percent of the bishops have felt strongly enough about an issue to engage in a social or political protest. And 8 percent say they have engaged in civil disobedience.

Table 5.2

Percentage of Bishops who Have Engaged in Various Political Activities

Touched on controversial issue in sermon	99%
Taken public stand on a controversial issue	97
Written a letter to a public official	95
Written a letter to editor	76
Give sermons on politics	60
Signed or circulated a petition	59
Organized social or political study group	42
Engaged in protest demonstration	42
Issued pastoral letter on politics*	39
Given money to a candidate, party or PAC	25
Joined a political organization	19
Organized social or political organization	16
Engaged in civil disobedience	8
Taken public stand on candidate for office	5
Worked in a campaign	4
Endorsed a candidate from the pulpit	1

In this and subsequent tables which embrace multiple questions, n's may vary with respect to the number of bishops providing responses to individual questions. In this table n's range from 139 to 149.
* All auxiliary bishops answered "no" to this question, as they cannot issue pastoral letters.

While stressing a need to remain nonpartisan, many bishops endorse the idea of an active clergy. Since 1970, the bishops have become more supportive of clerical activism. In his 1970 study of Catholic priests in the United States, Andrew Greeley found that 54 percent of bishops agreed with the following statement: "Priests who feel called to do so ought to be witnessing to Christ on the picket line or speaking out on controversial issues."[59] In our sample, 75 percent of the bishops agree (see Table 5.3). There is no way of telling from this study, however, the personal sentiments of the bishops on Pope John Paul II's ban on clerics serving in public office.

POLITICAL ATTITUDES

Classifying the bishops' political attitudes is not simple. While bishops are liberal on some issues, they are conservative on others. Consistent with the general tone of the bishops' pastoral letters since the Council, the American hierarchy is liberal on many economic and foreign policy issues. There exists greater disagreement, however, on social issues, including the Equal Rights Amendment, affirmative action, and whether homosexuals should be allowed to teach in the public schools.

Table 5.3
Bishops' Attitudes on Political Activism of Clergy (Percentages)

	AGREE STRONGLY	AGREE	DISAGREE	DISAGREE STRONGLY
"Priests who feel called to do so ought to be witnessing to Christ on the picket line or speaking out on controversial issues"	9	67	22	3
"Clergymen of different faiths need to cooperate more in politics, even if they cannot agree on theology"	11	73	14	2
"The primary task of the Church is to encourage its members to live the Christian life rather than to try to reform world"	9	36	45	10

n's range from 136 to 142.

When asked to classify their own political views, 25 percent of bishops say they are "liberal" or "very liberal," while only 14 percent identify themselves as "conservatives." Sixty-one percent describe their views as "middle-of-the-road." Fifty-two percent of the bishops say they identify with the Democratic party, while 23 percent identify with the Republicans. The bishops' support for the Democratic party exemplifies a historically strong association between American Catholics and the Democratic party. This association, reinforced in the election of 1960, goes back to days when Catholic immigrants from Europe found refuge in the Democratic party.[60]

Not unlike many Americans, a sizable percentage of bishops express no partisanship.[61] Twenty-five percent identify as independents or nonpartisans.

ECONOMIC ISSUES

Since medieval times, Catholic social teaching has given endorsement to the use of government power to regulate the economy. In his controversial classic *The Protestant Ethic and the Spirit of Capitalism*, Max Weber argued that Catholic attitudes toward the economy differ in fundamental ways from those emphasized by the Protestantism that grew from the Reformation.[62] Protestant theology, he maintained, is more conducive to the development of free market capitalism.

Table 5.4
Bishops' Support for Selected Economic and Government Policies
(Percentages)

	Favor	Oppose
Federal health insurance for all persons	94%	6%
Less government regulation of business	53	47
Nationalization of selected basic industries	16	84
Intensified federal efforts to eliminate poverty	97	3
Reducing the size of government	88	12
A guaranteed annual income	61	39
Shifting power from federal to state/local government	70	30
A crackdown on welfare recipients	16	84
Tax shift so that burden falls more heavily on corporations and persons with large incomes	94	6
More government spending on social programs	89	11

n's range from 131 to 146.

Especially since the publication of Pope Leo XIII's encyclical on labor conditions during the Industrial Revolution, popes have stressed a need for governments to regulate capitalism.[63] *Rerum novarum* (The condition of Labor), published in 1891, was the first in a series of papal encyclicals outlining Catholic teaching on capitalism, socialism, and communism.[64]

As the Church put it at the Second Vatican Council, "The growing complexity of modern situations makes it necessary for public authority to intervene more often in social, cultural and economic matters in order to bring about more favorable conditions to enable citizens and groups to pursue freely and effectively the achievement of man's well-being in its totality."[65]

Consistent with the tone of papal encyclicals and the bishops' own pastoral letter, "Economic Justice for All," support among the bishops for government programs is strong. Better than 90 percent of the bishops support programs of national health insurance, progressive taxation, and intensified federal efforts to eliminate poverty (see Table 5.4). But while the bishops endorse additional governmental programs, a large majority support a reduction in the size of government. For some, this apparent inconsistency in attitudes is attributable to a lack of political sophistication and ignorance of issues.[66]

Bishops educated on the social encyclicals of the last two centuries, however, can find justification for both positions. While the Church urged greater government control over the economy, it likewise warned against an overconcentration of power. Condemning communism and fascism for restricting religious and political freedom, the Church has been on both sides of the question of governmental power. Popes Leo XIII and Pius XI endorsed a "principle of subsidiarity" that requires that government intrusion be limited to the extent necessary to alleviate the problem and that government not excessively restrict individual freedom.

The bishops are also products of American culture. American bishops express the ambivalent attitudes toward government that permeate American society.[67] Speaking out on the dangers of excessive bureaucracy, American bishops in 1922 wrote,

The growth of bureaucracy . . . must be resolutely checked. Federal assistance and federal direction are in some cases beneficial and even necessary, but extreme bureaucracy is foreign to everything American. It is unconstitutional and undemocratic. It means officialism, red tape, and prodigal waste of public money. It spells hordes of so-called experts and self-perpetuating cliques of politicians to regulate every detail of daily life. It would eventually sovietize our form of government.[68]

Despite charges that the bishops' economic pastoral is antibusiness, the bishops are split on their view of government regulation of business. Fifty-three percent of the bishops actually favor less regulation of business.

FOREIGN POLICY AND DEFENSE

As late as 1965, Cardinal Spellman typified the Catholic cleric intensely supportive of U.S. foreign policy. In response to a reporter's request for his views on U.S. involvement in Vietnam, Spellman declared, "I fully support everything it does. . . . My country, may it always be right. Right or wrong, my country."[69]

As Dorothy Dohen points out, the American hierarchy supported every American war before 1968.[70] But as the war in Vietnam wore on, support gradually waned. Stopping short of formally opposing the war, the bishops began to offer tentative criticism as early as 1968.[71] By 1971, the bishops demanded an end to the war:

At this point in history, it seems clear to us that whatever good we hope to achieve through continued involvement in this war is now outweighed by the destruction of human life and of moral values which it inflicts. It is our firm conviction, therefore, that the speedy ending of this war is a moral imperative of the highest priority. Hence, we feel a moral obligation to appeal urgently to our

Table 5.5
Bishops' Support for Foreign and Defense-Related Policies (Percentages)

	Favor	Oppose
U.S. withdrawal from overseas commitments	26%	74%
Economic sanctions against South Africa	77	23
Nuclear Weapons Freeze	79	21
Use of U.S. troops to prevent communist takeover in El Salvador	18	82
Increase in defense spending	11	89

n's range from 138 to 141.

Table 5.6
Bishops' Responses to Foreign Policy and Defense-Related Statements (Percentages)

	AGREE	DISAGREE
It is sometimes necessary for the CIA to undermine hostile governments	21%	79%
We should be more forceful with the USSR even at risk of war	15	85
American military should be the strongest no matter what the cost	13	87
The powers of the United Nations ought to be strengthened	84	16
U.S. is morally obligated to prevent destruction of Israel	31	69
The use of violence is sometimes justified in bringing an end to social and economic oppression	44	56

n's range from 136 to 141.

nation's leaders and indeed to the leaders of all the nations involved in this tragic conflict to bring the war to an end with no further delay.[72]

The pastoral letter on nuclear weapons, "Challenge of Peace," is indicative of the major shift in the bishops' views on foreign and defense policy.[73] Many bishops are moving toward liberal positions, as Table 5.5 suggests. An overwhelming majority endorse a nuclear weapons freeze and cuts in defense spending. By better than three to one, bishops endorse the use of economic sanctions against South Africa. By a similar margin they oppose using the Central Intelligence Agency to undermine hostile governments.

Consistent with papal and conciliar endorsements of the United Nations, 84 percent of bishops agree that the powers of the United Nations ought to be strengthened (see Table 5.6).

Bishops are most divided on the use of violence as a means to bring an end to social and economic oppression. Controversy over liberation theology, which justifies the use of violence to end the domination of the rich in Latin America, has been troubling for the Church and Rome. It is an issue that deeply divides many Catholics.

SOCIAL ISSUES

While the bishops overwhelmingly support greater controls and restrictions on abortion, on other issues generally considered part of the agenda of the religious Right, the bishops are not predominantly conservative. The bishops are split over the Equal Rights Amendment (ERA), affirmative action, and whether to allow homosexuals to teach in the schools.

The ERA poses a problem for many bishops, who fear that such an amendment to the Constitution may give greater legal support for abortion. While the bishops have gone on record stating, "We will support legislation and affirmative action laws that assure women equal opportunity and treatment and that remove sex discrimination," they have withheld official support for the ERA.[74] "As a body the bishops have not been able to support the Equal Rights Amendment in its present form without a guarantee that the ERA will not be interpreted as securing the right to abortion as public policy," they maintain.[75] Nevertheless, 42 percent say they favor the amendment.

On issues of civil rights, bishops are strongly supportive of minority concerns. The bishops are nearly unanimous in supporting "stepped-up efforts at achieving racial equality," as Table 5.7 indicates. When put more specifically, nearly half of the bishops believe that special hiring preference should be given to blacks (see Table 5.8). (Twenty-nine percent support such special treatment for women.) Sixty-four percent support the use of busing if necessary to integrate the schools.

On whether or not homosexuals should be allowed to teach in the public schools, the bishops are divided. Fifty-six percent disagree with the statement that "homosexuals should not teach in public schools."

A majority of the bishops in 1974 went on record opposing capital punishment.[76] In 1980 they presented a more detailed statement outlining their reasons for opposing the death penalty.[77] But in the document they acknowledge that a position supporting the use of capital punishment is not incompatible with Catholic tradition. While most bishops, consistent with pastoral statements, oppose the death penalty, 19 percent say they do favor the "death penalty for first degree murderers."

Table 5.7
Bishops' Support for Selected Social, Environmental, and Law Enforcement Policy Issues (Percentages)

	Favor	Oppose
Stepped-up efforts at achieving racial equality	98%	2%
Integrating schools by busing if necessary	64	36
Greater abortion controls and restrictions	96	4
The Equal Rights Amendment	42	58
Legalized gambling	22	78
Tuition tax credits	98	2
School prayer amendment	69	31
Stepped-up efforts to preserve wilderness	93	7
Greater government efforts to control pollution	92	8
Accelerated nuclear energy development	52	48
Ban on handguns	92	8
Greater government efforts to curb marijuana use	90	10
Less lenient treatment of criminals	51	49
Death penalty for first degree murderers	19	81

n's range from 131 to 144.

Table 5.8
Bishops' Responses to Selected Statements on Social Policy and Family-Related Issues (Percentages)

	AGREE	DISAGREE
Special preference should be given to hiring women	29%	71%
Special preference should be given to hiring blacks	49	51
Women with young children should not work unless necessary	80	20
Homosexuals should not teach in public schools	44	56

n's range from 138 to 143.

Nearly one-third of the bishops say they oppose a school prayer amendment. There are several possible explanations for this position. While some bishops may oppose the amendment citing a need to keep church and state separate, opposition might also stem from a belief that such an amendment would not go far enough. The bishops also seek to have religious instruction given in the public schools. In their 1973 statement, the bishops argue, "An amendment permitting religious instruction and prayer in public schools and other public institutions is vitally important to protect the religious liberty of parents and children." They stress that "an amendment limited to allowing prayer would be inadequate to meet the national need."[78]

OPINION DIFFERENCES AMONG THE BISHOPS

While overall the bishops are generally liberal, differences of opinion within the hierarchy are evident. These political differences among America's Catholic bishops contribute to tensions within the hierarchy. Not all bishops are comfortable with the level of political activism in the Church since the Second Vatican Council. Some would prefer that more attention be given to internal church matters. Others simply disagree with policy positions endorsed in the pastoral letters of the NCCB. The following sections investigate the political variability among bishops on several dimensions.

The Irish Factor

Historically the American clergy has been dominated by Irishmen. In order to overcome the shortage of priests in the early American Church, many foreign-born priests were brought to America. Ireland, which had an abundance of priests, was a natural recruiting ground. By 1900, 62 percent of bishops in the United States were Irish.[79]

The Irish wing of the clergy has had close ties with Rome and has been relatively conservative politically.[80] In our sample, Irish bishops are somewhat different from their non-Irish counterparts. While Irish bishops are more likely to describe themselves as politically liberal (28 to 21 percent), they are less likely to identify themselves as Democrats (47 to 54 percent). While on most issue positions, Irish and non-Irish bishops are very similar, one exception is the issue of women's rights.

On the question of support for the Equal Rights Amendment, Irish bishops are more conservative. Forty-nine percent of non-Irish bishops, but only 34 percent of Irish bishops, support the ERA. One explanation for this may be that many of the more recently appointed non-Irish bishops that come from ethnic minority groups may be more sympathetic to the issue of women's rights. More important, however, may be the age differences between Irish and non-Irish bishops. While slightly more than one-half (51 percent) of non-Irish bishops are over the age of sixty, better than 78 percent of Irish bishops are over sixty. Older bishops might be expected to hold more traditional views with regard to women. Forty-two percent of bishops under sixty disagree with the statement that "women with young children should not work outside the home," while only 15 percent of bishops over sixty disagree.

Table 5.9
Bishops' Activity on Peace or Economy Pastorals by Support for Selected
Public Policies (Percentage Favoring)

	Active (n=91)	Not Active (n=56)
Less government regulation of business	48%	62%
Shifting power from federal to state/local government	61	86
Increase in social spending	92	82
The Equal Rights Amendment	43	39
Economic sanctions against South Africa	80	69
Nuclear Weapons Freeze	83	71
Death penalty for first degree murderers	13	30
School prayer amendment	61	81

Table 5.10
Bishops' Level of Activity on Peace or Economy Pastorals by
Self-Described Political Views (Percentages)

	Liberal	Middle of the Road	Conservative
Active (n=91)	32%	60%	8%
Not Active (n=53)	15	60	25

Table 5.11
Bishops' Level of Activity on Peace or Economy Pastorals by Party
Preference (Percentages)

	Democrat	Independent/None	Republican
Active (n=88)	58%	24%	18%
Not Active (n=52)	42	25	33

Participation in Writing Economic and Peace Pastorals

All bishops under the retirement age of seventy-five are members of the NCCB, but some bishops are more active in the organization. Our data (summarized in Tables 5.9, 5.10, and 5.11) suggest political differences between those who took an active part in the drafting of one or both of the pastorals on peace and the economy and those who did not.[81] In the view of one bishop who did not participate in developing the pastorals, "Bishops should stay out of politics." They "can't and should not try to control Catholics and their political leanings."

The literature is mixed on whether political actives among the clergy tend toward liberal or conservative politics. In his study of Protestant clergy, Jeffrey Hadden finds politically active clergy to be more liberal than their fellow clerics, who concern themselves primarily with church matters.[82] Harold Quinley finds similar results in his study of Protestant ministers in California.[83] Studies of fundamentalist clergy, however, show much greater support for political action on the part of conservative ministers.[84]

The nature of the issues may be the important factor determining whether conservative or liberal clerics will engage in political activism. Hadden and Quinley studied ministers during a period when civil rights and Vietnam War protests were at the forefront of the national political agenda. The increased political activism on the part of conservative, fundamentalist clergy coincides with an ascendance to the national political debate of issues such as school prayer and abortion.

Since the United States Supreme Court decision in *Webster*, the American Catholic bishops have sensed an opening in influencing the abortion debate. Bishops strongly committed to church teaching on abortion but perhaps less committed to the progressive agenda endorsed by the NCCB in the 1980s may be more motivated to speak out now. With the placement of abortion atop the bishops' agenda, more conservative prelates are assuming leadership roles in the political fight.

The data suggest that differences exist between those who actively participated in the writing of the political pastorals on peace and the economy and those who did not. Those who took a more active role are more likely to support the social action and liberal positions to which the bishops addressed themselves.

When comparing bishops who were active in drafting one or both of the recent pastorals on peace and the economy with those who were not active, we found the actives to be more liberal, in terms of both self-descriptions and support for specific policies. The actives are also more likely to identify with the Democratic party.

It may be that conservative bishops simply opt out of a process they see leading to policy recommendations with which they may not agree or upon which they feel they cannot have an influence. As French Cardinal Paul Gouyon writes of the episcopal conference:

A relatively significant number of bishops never express themselves during the plenary sessions. Some, who during the early years of their participation readily took the floor, simply have decided now not to intervene any longer. . . . Once the general meeting is adjourned, the bishop returns to his own diocese. Some powerful structures, administrative boards, commissions, and departments supply him with information on all the problems about which he can hope to be enlightened, but in the face of which he is defenseless. . . . The bishop feels himself inferior to these commissions and only participates in one of them. . . . Thus, the temptation to take refuge in silence even if he is vaguely aware of being out of step.[85]

Many bishops who may not have felt compelled to actively participate in the debate on the progressive economic and peace agenda may be somewhat more sympathetic to the abortion cause. These bishops often are viewed more highly by Rome.

Papal Bias in the Selection of Bishops

Despite those who call for the use of more democratic procedures in the selection of bishops, the process of episcopal appointments is dominated by the pope. Under the reign of Pope John Paul II, an increasing number of conservative clerics are being appointed as new bishops. In an effort to check the decline in American Catholics' obedience to official church teaching on the use of artificial birth control and abortion, John Paul is seeking out bishops who will stress church teaching on these issues. In a statement indicative of this position, one bishop appointed by John Paul states, "I am happy with the Bishops' involvement in major issues that affect our national life," but "I do believe it is time for us to concentrate more on catechetics and internal Church matters [and] I would like more attention and support given to the pro-life movement."

To control for papal appointment, the sample was broken down by years as bishop. Those serving from zero to nine years are bishops appointed during the reign of Pope John Paul II. Those serving between ten and twenty-five years were appointed during the reign of Pope Paul VI. To illustrate the variance among John Paul II's most recent appointees, Tables 5.12, 5.13, and 5.14 differentiate between the first and second halves of John Paul's tenure.

Differences in views toward Vatican II separate recent appointees and older bishops. Lending some support to the notion that recently appointed bishops are less committed to changes stressed by the Council, newer bishops were found to be more content with the status quo. When asked to express their view on the Council, 34 percent of all bishops say the Church has "not gone far enough" in implementing the social and political

Table 5.12
Years as Bishop by Attitudes Toward the Implementation of Social and Political Teachings of Vatican II (Percentages)

	Gone Too Far	About Right	Not Far Enough
0-4 (n=14)	0%	86%	14%
5-9 (n=33)	3	61	36
10-24 (n=77)	1	61	38
25+ (n=25)	0	72	28

Table 5.13
Years as Bishop by Self-Described Political Views (Percentages)

	Liberal	Middle of the Road	Conservative
0-4 (n=14)	7%	64%	29%
5-9 (n=33)	21	67	12
10-24 (n=75)	35	52	13
25+ (n=24)	13	79	8

Table 5.14
Years as Bishop by Party Preference (Percentages)

	Democrat	Independent/None	Republican
0-4 (n=13)	38%	23%	38%
5-9 (n=32)	56	22	22
10-24 (n=75)	59	24	17
25+ (n=23)	30	35	35

teachings of Vatican II. Of those bishops appointed since 1985, only 14 percent feel this way.

Those bishops appointed by Pope Paul VI are more likely to be self-described liberals and Democrats than are those appointed by Pope John Paul II. The differences are most pronounced among those elevated within the last five years. This lag may be explained by the institutional sluggishness of the church bureaucracy. It may take an incoming pontiff several months or years to put his men into place in the recruitment bureaucracy.

Greater differences among the most recent appointees may also be indicative of intensified efforts in Rome to appoint more conservative clerics after American bishops tilted left in their pastoral letters on nuclear weapons and the economy. Rome is concerned with the direction of the American Church, which it sees as overly permissive. New bishops, committed to greater discipline, are sought to stem the tide.

CONCLUSION

Through the unprecedented activism of the National Conference of Catholic Bishops during the 1980s, American Catholic bishops assumed a position as chief religious commentators on American politics. Offering extensively researched statements on nuclear weapons and the economy, the bishops became major players in the national political debate.

In the 1990s, NCCB priorities are shifting as the bishops commit increased time and resources toward efforts to ban legalized abortion. Emphasizing church authority and strict obedience, their tactics are in stark contrast to the consultative processes reminiscent of the eighties.

Some bishops are concerned that an authoritarian approach is out of date in a post–Vatican II, pluralistic America. But bishops comfortable with the old style are assuming new leadership positions.

Differences of opinion within the American hierarchy offer insight into the current policy shifts at the NCCB. Though America's bishops are often referred to as if they are a unified bloc, significant disagreement exists among them. Consistent with conventional wisdom, most American bishops are liberal on economic and foreign policy issues. Their support for the Democratic party is congruent with their self-described liberal views. But conventional wisdom errs in assuming bishops are conservative on social issues. Better than 40 percent favor the Equal Rights Amendment, 56 percent believe that homosexuals should be allowed to teach in the schools, and 64 percent support busing to integrate the schools. Differences in attitudes toward the implementation of Vatican II also divide the bishops. One-third of the bishops believe that the Church has not gone far enough in carrying out the political and social teachings of Vatican II.

As the national policy agenda shifts, however, so too does the bishops' agenda.[86] The bishops' pastoral letter on nuclear weapons is less immediately relevant as communism falls in Eastern Europe and more cordial relations between the United States and Russia are fostered. As the Reagan assault on government welfare programs has ended, issues stressed in "Economic Justice for All" command less attention. Supreme Court decisions allowing some state restrictions on the abortion right, however, are refocusing public debate. And bishops sense an opportunity to address a salient issue.

Since the Church's position on abortion demands strict obedience, those bishops preferring stricter discipline are more comfortable with the current direction of the NCCB. Many of the same bishops who may not have been moved to engage in the debate on "Challenge of Peace" and "Economic Justice for All" now have an issue that they deem more deserving of the bishops' attention. These bishops tend toward greater political conservatism. And there are an increasing number of them.

In the United States, Pope John Paul II's episcopal appointees are more likely to be Republican and politically conservative than those bishops appointed by Pope Paul VI. They are more committed to greater discipline within the Church and are less concerned with pushing farther the reforms of Vatican II.

The institutional structure of the Roman Catholic Church affords one of the most ordered and effective bureaucracies the world has ever seen. The papacy dominates the institution. Vatican II emphasized the communal dimensions of Catholicism and a need for bishops and the laity to play a greater role in the development of church policy. Thirty years after the Council, however, the primacy of the papacy endures. The power exercised by the pope in the selection of bishops allows the pontiff opportunities to redirect the church hierarchy. Not unlike the political criteria American presidents apply when appointing Supreme Court justices, the pope demands certain qualities from an episcopal candidate, including a political outlook consistent with that of the Vatican.

The papacies of Popes Paul VI and John Paul II differ in important ways. As pontiff during the final years of Vatican II, Paul appointed bishops strongly committed to the politically progressive agenda associated with the Second Vatican Council. Support for social and political action to address the problems of poverty, war, and civil rights was a characteristic more often found among Paul's appointees. Concern for the maintenance of church authority and Catholic obedience to church teaching has been stressed more prominently during the reign of John Paul II. Seeking bishops firmly committed to church teaching on birth control, divorce, priest celibacy, and an all-male clergy, Pope John Paul II has appointed bishops who are politically conservative as well.

While a return to pre–Vatican II ways seems improbable given the strong commitment American bishops and the Catholic laity have to the

Council, attempts to enforce authoritarian controls in a pluralistic society could backfire.[87] When stressing church social teaching on economic and foreign policy issues, bishops have had a receptive audience among lay Catholics.[88] But on issues of sexual morality and abortion, American Catholics are much less likely to agree with church teaching.[89]

Bishops are not likely to shy away from politics. They forcefully demand the right to engage in the political debate. But the nature of that involvement is changing as the current pope seeks new bishops strictly obedient to Rome and American prelates commit themselves to the dogmatic teaching on abortion.

While the bishops' involvement in politics will continue to be cyclical as issues change, less certain is whether the bishops will be able to command the attention they did in the 1980s or will simply embark upon an era in which they dialogue only among themselves.

NOTES

1. National Conference of Catholic Bishops, "The Challenge of Peace: God's Promise and Our Response" (Washington, D.C.: United States Catholic Conference, 1983), and "Economic Justice for All: Catholic Social Teaching and the U.S. Economy" (Washington, D.C.: United States Catholic Conference, 1986).

2. For collections of critical essays on the bishops' letters see Judith A. Dwyer, ed., *The Catholic Bishops and Nuclear War: A Critique and Analysis of the Pastoral "The Challenge of Peace"* (Washington, D.C.: Georgetown University Press, 1984), and Robert Royal, ed., *Challenge and Response: Critiques of the Catholic Bishops' Draft Letter on the U.S. Economy*, vol. 57, February 1985 (Washington, D.C.: Ethics and Public Policy Center, 1985).

3. Francis X. Winters, "Bishops and Scholars: The Peace Pastoral under Siege," *Review of Politics* 48, no. 1 (Winter 1986), p. 31.

4. Dinesh D'Souza, "The Bishops as Pawns: Behind the Scenes at the U.S. Catholic Conference," *Policy Review* (Fall 1985), p. 51.

5. See, for example, George A. Kelly, *The Crisis of Authority* (Chicago: Regnery Gateway, 1982); Philip Lawler, *How Bishops Decide* (Washington, D.C.: Ethics and Public Policy Center, 1986); Avery Dulles, "The Teaching Authority of the Bishops' Conference," *America*, June 11, 1983, pp. 453–455.

6. "U.S. Bishops Reject Bid by Vatican to Curb Role," *New York Times*, November 17, 1988; "American Bishops to Explain Range of Positions to Pope," *San Francisco Chronicle*, March 8, 1989. See also Penny Lernoux, *People of God: The Struggle for World Catholicism* (New York: Viking, 1989), chap. 8.

7. Quoted in Peter Steinfels, "Bishop Lends Ear to Ideas on Abortion," *New York Times*, March 27, 1990, p. A9.

8. Quoted in Pat Windsor, "Cincinnati Prelate with a 'German Soul' Leads U.S. Bishops," *National Catholic Reporter*, June 15, 1990, p. 8.

9. Administrative Board of the United States Catholic Conference, "Political Responsibility: Choices for the 1980s," October 26, 1979, in Hugh J. Nolan, ed., *Pastoral Letters of the United States Catholic Bishops*, vol. 4 (Washington, D.C.: United States Catholic Conference, 1984), p. 319.

10. John Tracy Ellis, *American Catholicism*, 2nd ed. (Chicago: University of Chicago Press, 1969), p. 74.

11. Fourth Provincial Council of Baltimore, "Pastoral Letter," May 23, 1840, in Nolan, *Pastoral Letters*, vol. 1, p. 133.

12. Ibid., p. 134.

13. Quoted in Daniel Callahan, *The Mind of the Catholic Layman* (New York: Scribner's, 1963), p. 13.

14. This term was used by Monsignor John Tracy Ellis to place part of the responsibility on Catholics for the economic and social disadvantages they suffered in America. See John Tracy Ellis, *American Catholics and the Intellectual Life* (Chicago: Heritage Foundation, 1956), p. 57.

15. Andrew M. Greeley, *The American Catholic: A Social Portrait* (New York: Basic Books, 1977), p. 20.

16. James M. Penning, "The Political Behavior of American Catholics: An Assessment of the Impact of Group Integration vs. Group Identification," *Western Political Quarterly* 41, no. 2 (June 1988), pp. 289–308.

17. Ellis, *American Catholicism*, p. 105.

18. David C. Leege, "Catholics and the Civic Order: Parish Participation, Politics, and Civic Participation," *The Review of Politics* 50, no. 4 (Fall 1988), pp. 704–736.

19. For a history of the origins of this organization, see Elizabeth McKeown, "The National Bishops' Conference: An Analysis of Its Origins," *Catholic Historical Review* 66 (October 1980), pp. 565–576.

20. Quoted in ibid., pp. 574–575.

21. For the arguments of Bishop Charles E. McDonnell of Brooklyn and Cardinal William O'Connell of Boston, see ibid.

22. Administrative Committee of the National Catholic War Council, "Program of Social Reconstruction," February 12, 1919, in Nolan, *Pastoral Letters*, vol. 1, pp. 255–271.

23. Ibid., p. 265.

24. Quoted in Ellis, *American Catholicism*, p. 145.

25. Ibid.

26. Quoted in Gerald P. Fogarty, ed., *Patterns of Episcopal Leadership* (New York: Macmillan, 1989), p. 169.

27. Quoted in Edward Duff, "The Church and American Public Life," in Philip Gleason, ed., *Contemporary Catholicism in the United States* (Notre Dame, Ind.: University of Notre Dame Press, 1969), p. 107

28. U.S. Catholic Bishops, "Discrimination and Christian Conscience," November 14, 1958, in Nolan, *Pastoral Letters*, vol. 2, pp. 201–206.

29. Quoted in Thomas J. Shelley, "Paul J. Hallinan," in Fogarty, *Patterns of Episcopal Leadership*, p. 247.

30. See Stephen Ochs, *Desegregating the Altar: The Josephites and the Struggle for Black Priests, 1871–1960* (Baton Rouge: Louisiana State University Press, 1990).

31. David O'Brien argues that the bishops developed a more "republican" style of leadership in contrast to the "immigrant" style that marked the actions of men like Spellman. Not confined to addressing the issues of Catholics alone, the bishops have attempted to make religious and political appeals to the entire nation. They now see themselves as mainstream members of the American republic. (David O'Brien, *Public Catholicism* [New York: Macmillan, 1989]).

32. Vatican Council II, *Christus dominus* October 28, 1965, in Austin P. Flannery, ed., *Documents of Vatican II* (Grand Rapids, Mich.: Eerdmans, 1975), p. 570.

33. Ibid., pp. 574–575, par. 18.

34. See Greeley, *The American Catholic*.

35. See "Bishops Warn Politicians on Abortion," *New York Times*, November 8, 1989, p. A10.

36. Webster v. Reproductive Health Services 109 U.S. 304 (1989).

37. See Steinfels, "Bishop Lends Ear to Ideas on Abortion," p. A9; "Flexibility Urged on Abortion Issue," *New York Times*, May 21, 1990, p. A13; and Mary Gorski, "Weakland Urges Abortion Shifts," *National Catholic Reporter*, June 1, 1990, p. 1.

38. Richard P. McBrien, "A Papal Attack on Vatican II," *New York Times*, March 12, 1990, p. A15; "Theologians Challenge Vatican's Conservative Style," *Sacramento Bee*, July 22, 1989, p. AA8.

39. See Martin Smith, "Retrogressive Bishops," *Sacramento Bee*, November 20, 1989, p. B4.

40. Excerpt from interview with *National Catholic Reporter*, January 12, 1990, p. 24.

41. See for example Dorothy Dohen, *Nationalism and American Catholicism (New York: Oxford University Press, 1968)*.

42. Eugene C. Kennedy and Victor J. Heckler, *The Catholic Priest in the United States: Psychological Investigations* (Washington, D.C.: United States Catholic Conference, 1972), p. 216.

43. For a good review of the problems involved, see James A. Bill and Robert L. Hardgrave, Jr., *Comparative Politics: The Quest for Theory* (Lanham, Md.: University Press of America, 1981), chap. 5.

44. Reported in Mary T. Hanna, *Catholics and American Politics* (Cambridge, Mass.: Harvard University Press, 1979).

45. Ibid.

46. Thomas J. Reese, *Archbishop: Inside the Power Structure of the American Catholic Church* (New York: Harper and Row, 1989).

47. Ibid., p. 317.

48. Thomas J. Reese, "A Survey of the American Bishops," *America*, November 12, 1983, pp. 285–288.

49. Andrew M. Greeley, *The Catholic Priest in the United States: Sociological Investigations* (Washington, D.C.: United States Catholic Conference, 1972).

50. Robert Lerner, Stanley Rothman, and S. Robert Lichter, "Christian Religious Elites," *Public Opinion* (March/April 1989), pp. 54–59.

51. See Reese, "A Survey of the American Bishops," p. 286.

52. In a 1970 survey, 94 percent of bishops said their thinking has been influenced "greatly" by the documents of Vatican II. See Greeley, *The Catholic Priest in the United States*, p. 188.

53. See Lernoux, *People of God,* chaps. 7, 8.

54. Many bishops are uncomfortable using terms such as "politics" and "political" when describing their activities. Use of such terms in this study are in no way meant to be disrespectful to the bishops, but are used to convey accepted understandings to fellow political scientists.

55. Vatican Council II, *Gaudium et spes*, December 7, 1965, in Flannery, *Documents,* p. 947, par. 44.

56. Ibid., p. 964, par. 60.

57. Ibid., p. 982, par. 75.

58. "Political Responsibility: Choices for the 1980s," October 26, 1979, in Nolan, *Pastoral Letters*, vol. 4, pp. 317–329.

59. Greeley, *The Catholic Priest in the United States*, p. 97.

60. For a historical overview of the association of Catholics with the Democratic party see Hanna, *Catholics and American Politics*; Jay P. Dolan, *The American Catholic Experience: A History from Colonial Times to the Present* (Garden City, N.Y.: Doubleday, 1985); and James A. Reichley, *Religion in American Public Life* (Washington, D.C.: The Brookings Institution, 1985), chap. 5.

61. See, for example, David S. Broder, *The Party's Over* (New York: Harper and Row, 1972); William Crotty and Gary Jacobson, *American Parties in Decline*, 2nd ed. (Boston: Little, Brown, 1984); Helmut Norpoth and Jerrold G. Rusk, "Partisan Dealignment in the American Electorate: Itemizing the Deductions since 1964," *American Political Science Review* 76 (September 1982), pp. 522–537; Martin P. Wattenberg, *The Decline of American Political Parties, 1952–1984* (Cambridge, Mass.: Harvard University Press, 1986).

62. Max Weber, *The Protestant Ethic and the Spirit of Capitalism* (New York: Scribner's, 1958).

63. Leo XIII, *Rerum novarum*, May 15, 1891.

64. Papal encyclical outcomes on economics since *Rerum novarum* include Pius XI, *Quadragesimo anno*, May 15, 1931; John XXIII, *Mater et magistra*, 1961, and *Pacem in terris*, 1963; Paul VI, *Populorum progressio*, 1967, and apostolic letter *Octogesima adveniens*, 1971; John Paul II, *Laborem exercens*, September 14, 1981, *Sollicitudo rei socialis*, December 30, 1987, and *Centesimuss annus*, May 1, 1991.

65. Vatican Council II, *Gaudium et spes*, in Flannery, *Documents*, p. 983, par. 75.

66. For debate over the level of ideological constraint among voters, see Philip E. Converse, "The Nature of Belief Systems in Mass Publics," in David Apter, ed., *Ideology and Discontent* (New York: Free Press, 1964), and the subsequent literature, including Norman Nie and Kristi Anderson, "Mass Belief Systems Revisited: Political Change and Attitude Structure," *Journal of Politics* 36, no. 3 (August 1974), pp. 540–591, and Hugh L. LeBlanc and Mary Beth Merrin, "Mass Belief Systems Revisited," *Journal of Politics* 39, no. 4 (November 1977), pp. 1082–1087. For an evaluation of the bishops' understanding of issues, see D'Souza, "The Bishops as Pawns."

67. For an excellent study on the dimensions of public attitudes toward capitalism and democracy, see Herbert McClosky and John Zaller, *The American Ethos: Public Attitudes toward Capitalism and Democracy* (Cambridge, Mass.: Harvard University Press, 1984).

68. Administrative Committee of the National Catholic Welfare Conference, "Statement on Federalization and Bureaucracy," January 26, 1922, in Nolan, *Pastoral Letters*, vol. 1, p. 334.

69. Quoted in Dohen, *Nationalism and American Catholicism*, p. 1.

70. Ibid.

71. National Conference of Catholic Bishops, "Human Life in Our Day," November 15, 1968, in Nolan, *Pastoral Letters*, vol. 3, pp. 182–194.

72. National Conference of Catholic Bishops, "Resolution on Southeast Asia," November 1971, in Nolan, *Pastoral Letters*, vol. 3, p. 289.

73. National Conference of Catholic Bishops, "The Challenge of Peace: God's Promise and Our Response," May 3, 1983, in Nolan, *Pastoral Letters*, vol. 4, pp. 493–581.

74. U.S. Catholic Bishops, "Partners in the Mystery of Redemption: A Pastoral Response to Women's Concerns for Church and Society," first draft, in *Origins*, April 21, 1988, p. 776.

75. Ibid.; see bishops' footnote 109, pp. 786–787.

76. "Resolution Against Capital Punishment," November 18, 1974, in Nolan, *Pastoral Letters*, vol. 3, p. 464.

77. "Statement on Capital Punishment," November 1980, in Nolan, *Pastoral Letters*, vol. 4, pp. 427–434.

78. "Statement on Prayer and Religious Instruction in Public Schools," September 19, 1973, in Nolan, *Pastoral Letters*, vol. 3, pp. 378, 379.

79. Dolan, *The American Catholic Experience*, p. 143.

80. Edward Wakin and Joseph F. Scheuer, *The De-Romanization of the American Catholic Church* (New York: Macmillan, 1966).

81. While bishops on the drafting committees numbered only about fifteen, bishops were asked to classify their level of participation in the entire process, which could include debate, consultation, and so forth. Therefore, more bishops than those on the drafting committees played a role in the process.

82. Jeffrey K. Hadden, *The Gathering Storm in the Churches* (Garden City, N.Y.: Doubleday, 1969).

83. Harold E. Quinley, *The Prophetic Clergy: Social Activism among Protestant Ministers* (New York: Wiley, 1974).

84. Kathleen Murphy Beatty and Oliver Walter, "Fundamentalists, Evangelicals and Politics," *American Politics Quarterly* 16, no. 1 (January 1988), pp. 43–59, and "A Group Theory of Religion and Politics: The Clergy as Group Leaders," *Western Political Quarterly* 42, no. 1 (March 1989), pp. 129–146; James L. Guth, "Pastoral Politics in the 1988 Election: Protestant Clergy and Political Mobilization" (Paper presented at the 1989 Annual Meeting of the American Political Science Association, Atlanta, Georgia).

85. Quoted in Philip Lawler, *How Bishops Decide* (Washington, D.C.: Ethics and Public Policy Center, 1986), p. 40.

86. Timothy Byrnes argues that the shifting political agenda since the 1960s, especially the increased federal role in the areas of social and economic policy, helped encourage American bishops to speak out more on these issues. See Timothy A. Byrnes, *Catholic Bishops in American Politics* (Princeton: Princeton University Press, 1991).

87. For evidence of lay Catholic support for the Second Vatican Council see Jim Castelli and Joseph Gremillion, *The Emerging Parish: The Notre Dame Study of Catholic Life since Vatican II* (San Francisco: Harper and Row, 1987), chap. 3.

88. See Leege, "Catholics and the Civic Order," and Joseph B. Tamney, Ronald Burton, and Stephen Johnson, "Christianity, Social Class, and the Catholic Bishops' Economic Policy," *Sociological Analysis* 49 (December 1988), pp. 78–96.

89. Greeley and Hout argue that the papal encyclical *Humanae Vitae* rather than Vatican II drove many Catholics away from Mass. (Andrew M. Greeley and Michael Hout, "The Center Doesn't Hold: Church Attendance in the United States, 1940–1984," *American Sociological Review* 52, no. 3 [June 1987], pp. 325–345.)

Chapter 6 _____

Religion, Politics, and the Catholic Laity

The extent to which Catholics are influenced by their bishops has been a question of much debate. Response to their bishops' political activities has been mixed. The evidence suggests that few Catholics are even aware of the bishops' pastoral letters, and the laity is in stark disagreement with the hierarchy on such issues as abortion, divorce, and birth control. But while abortion and sexual ethics are often emphasized as issues that separate Catholics from their leaders, these are only a few of many issues addressed by the bishops. Too much emphasis on disagreements over sexual ethics obscures areas of commonality. While most Catholics may not be conversant in the social teaching of their Church, the permeation of Vatican II ideas throughout Catholic culture may work to stem the movement of Catholics toward conservative politics. American Catholics have felt the pressures from a changing Church, changes that have moved Catholicism toward the politics of the Left. The politics of American Catholics and their response to their bishops must be viewed in this light.

CHANGING INFLUENCE OF RELIGION

In an increasingly secular age, it is difficult to know the extent to which religion still influences the social views of the people. As religious attachment declines, one might expect that religion would have a minimal impact on political attitudes. On the declining social influence of organized religion, Bryan Wilson writes, "Religion no longer explains the world, much less the cosmos, and its explanations of social phenomena are totally ignored; indeed when Catholic or Anglican archbishops today wish to pronounce on social affairs they rely neither on revelation or holy writ. They set up commissions, often with considerable reliance on the advice of sociologists."[1] While the decline in religious influence can be attributed to many factors including the elevation of science and the effects of modernization, some argue that religion itself has contributed to its own decline by contributing to the secularization of society. As Berger puts it, "Christianity has been its own grave digger."[2] Protestantism especially "was itself an agency of secularization, eliminating much of the previously established magic and mystery of the world."[3]

Some attribute an apparent decline in religiosity among Catholics to the effects of the Second Vatican Council. Michael Novak and James Hitchcock blame Vatican II for the falling away of the many Catholics who no longer attend church regularly.[4] Others argue that the loss of much church ritual and the relaxation of rules has left Catholics without clear, consistent behavioral guidelines and without a developed sense of connection to their fellow Catholics.[5]

Polls indicate that across Christian denominations there has been a decline since the 1950s in the number of those who say religion is very important in their lives. The number of Americans stating that religion is "very important" in their lives decreased from 75 percent in 1952 to 54 percent in 1988.[6] This decline has been especially evident among American Catholics. In 1952, 83 percent of Catholics said that religion was "very important" to them. By 1984 only 53 percent said the same.[7]

But church and synagogue attendance overall has not declined in the past fifty years. Gallup survey results illustrate a fairly stable rate of church attendance. In 1939, 41 percent attended church or synagogue in a typical week. In 1988, that figure stood at 42 percent.[8]

Among Catholics, however, church attendance has dropped off over the last two decades. While some have attributed this to the reforms of Vatican II, time series data between 1963 and 1974 suggest that church attendance actually rose after the Council, but began to decline after the issuance of *Humane vitae* in 1968.[9] It was in this document that Pope Paul VI reiterated the Church's ban on the use of artificial contraceptives. Since 1975, however, regular church attendance among Catholics has leveled off at about 50 percent. In Gallup surveys, Catholics who do not attend church regularly are most likely to cite church teaching on birth control and abortion and church authority as reasons for staying away.[10]

A decline in church attendance would not by itself necessarily imply an abandonment of religion. Even among those who do not attend church regularly, a belief in God is shared almost universally in American society. In fact, though there has been a decrease in church attendance among Catholics over the last forty years, most baptized Catholics still consider themselves to be church members.[11] While they may be less likely to follow the church obligation to attend Mass, they probably have not lost their attachment to religion. Religious beliefs may only be changing in form. In their study *Contrasting Values in Western Europe*, Harding, Phillips, and Fogarty found that "positive attitudes towards the institution of the church are separate from positive religious attitudes and acknowledgement of religious needs. . . . [A]spects concerned with feelings, experience, and the more numerous beliefs tend to cluster together, somewhat distinct from aspects involving ritual participation and institutional attachment."[12] Rather than abandoning religion, Europeans are becoming more pluralistic and tolerant in their religious beliefs. The secularizing tendencies, in other words, may not necessarily signify moral decline or a rejection of religion, but rather an acceptance of a different kind of religion, a more personal one.[13]

As W. C. Roof puts it, "The crucial question is not 'How *religious* is a person?' according to some preconceived culturally specific standards, but rather '*How* is the person religious?' "[14] For many individuals, a personalized faith has replaced institutional religion as a moral guide. In *The Invisible Religion*, Thomas Luckmann argues that often this personalized faith differs from the institutionalized form of religion. "The modern sacred cosmos legitimates the retreat of the individual into the 'private sphere' and sanctifies his subjective 'autonomy,' " he argues.[15] Hence, religion becomes more privatized. The "institutional specialization of religion, along with the specialization of other institutional areas, starts a development that transforms religion into an increasingly 'subjective' and 'private' reality."[16]

While this may mean that the laity is less willing to accept authority, it does not mean they have abandoned religion. Nurtured by the American cultural experience and encouraged by the Second Vatican Council, Catholics have a renewed sense of independence and personal confidence.

VATICAN II AND THE CATHOLIC LAITY

The post–Vatican II experience of greater lay participation in the Church is actually not without precedent in America. Lay power within the Church was more common in early America. When priests and bishops were in short supply, the clergy had to rely much more on the help from lay persons. As a consequence, the laity played a much larger role in church affairs.[17] This was nowhere more evident than under the system of lay trusteeism.

Lay trusteeism was a controversial system that greatly inflated the influence of lay Catholics. Until the 1860s, lay trustees were responsible for local church finances. This system was developed early in the colonial period when the Church was not permitted to hold property. To conform to state laws that recognized only specifically delegated members of congregations as rightful owners of church property, parish property was placed in the name of parishioners. This system generated opportunities for the laity to exert significant influence over parish decisions. Daniel Callahan argues that "this control was both a great opportunity and a great temptation to the layman. Lay trusteeism meant, on the one hand, that the layman was intimately involved in the running of the churches and, on the other, capable of creating havoc and disunity when he abused his power."[18]

The system was used by the laity as leverage in influencing clerical appointments, and it generated tension between church members and their bishops. According to Ellis, "The trouble arose when lay trustees took upon themselves the episcopal prerogative of appointing and dismissing their pastors. For the quarter century of John Carroll's rule and for years thereafter, this attempt on the part of laymen to usurp these rights was, perhaps, the most harassing problem with which the bishops had to deal in the United States."[19] And bishops fought back.

The system created problems for the hierarchy, which sought to maintain control. Daniel Callahan argues that "the trustee problem convinced the hierarchy that rigid discipline of both clergy and laity was absolutely essential."[20] The crackdown, however, came at the cost of suppressing the laity, at least until the Second Vatican Council. According to the former bishop of Reno, Robert J. Dwyer:

Trusteeism had to be crushed, no doubt about that. . . . But as in the case with almost every draconian measure, the rooting out of trusteeism meant also the damaging of the original American Catholic spirit. . . . Essential as was the victory for the divinely established authority of the bishops to rule their dioceses as successors of the Apostles, and not as chairmen of governing boards, it nevertheless resulted in a situation where the part of the laity in this cooperative effort which is the work of the Church was reduced to a minimum.[21]

By the 1840s the negative effects of trusteeism were abated.[22] The Church cracked down on lay participation with an authoritarianism that would last through the middle of the twentieth century. But things would change.

The Second Vatican Council gave lay Catholics new hope for a greater participatory role within the Church.[23] The Council sought to elevate the position of the laity by allowing them to participate more directly in the liturgy and in the decision-making process within the Church. Before Vatican II, the pomp and majesty surrounding the hierarchy encouraged Catholics to be deferential to authorities. A clear hierarchy of order was encouraged. When the Conference of English bishops met in February of 1966 to discuss how to implement the teachings of Vatican II, their first thought, wrote Bishop Augustine Harris, was, "How are we to persuade the laity not to kiss our episcopal rings any more?"[24] Instituting the reforms of the Council required bridging the gulf between the clergy and lay Catholics.

The elevated clergy to which so many Catholics had grown accustomed was reinforced by church liturgical practices, which identified the priest as the true agent of the liturgy.[25] The post–Vatican II change from the Latin Tridentine Mass to the Novas Ordo Mass (new rite) signified a major break from the past. The Latin Mass had remained essentially unchanged since the edict of Pope Pius V after the Council of Trent in 1570. In this ceremony the priest dominated. The laity was afforded few opportunities to participate in the Mass short of reciting fixed prayers. When the new Mass was introduced in 1969, stripping away much of the majesty of the older ceremony, traditionalists argued that these changes signified dangerous concessions to the secular world.[26] Many reasoned that such ritual change, by undermining the uniquely supernatural emphasis of the traditional Mass, would contribute to a further erosion of cultural religiosity and deference to church authority.[27]

Vatican II efforts to downplay differences between the laity and clergy raised questions about the effects on Catholics' attitudes toward their priests. Over the last twenty years, studies have documented a decline in the status of the clergy.[28] As William Dinges summarizes:

Vatican II had a dramatic impact on those at the core of the Church's institutional structure. *Aggiornamento* implicitly demythologized clerical life by weakening certain theological premises undergirding the clerical cultus. The Church was no longer to be defined exclusively in terms of clerical prerogatives. Laity were to become more integrated into Catholicism's institutional life. . . . This shift in the dispersion of sacred charisma raised ambiguities about the role of the priest as one who possessed exclusive mediational and sacred power.[29]

The Council told Catholics that they could not depend upon the clergy for guidance in all areas. "For guidance and spiritual strength let them turn to the clergy," the Council said, "but let them realize that their pastors will not always be so expert as to have a ready answer to every problem (even every grave problem) that arises; this is not the role of the clergy: it is rather up to the laymen to shoulder their responsibilities under the guidance of Christian wisdom and with eager attention to the teaching authority of the Church."[30] On many questions, answers are left to the individual's conscience.

In an effort to arrive at truth, the Council maintained that open inquiry would be necessary. "For the proper exercise of this role, the faithful, both clerical and lay, should be accorded a lawful freedom of inquiry, of thought, and of expression, tempered by humility and courage in whatever branch of study they have specialized."[31] By endorsing the principle of open inquiry and debate, however, the Church risked invoking more vigorous demands by the laity to have a voice within the Church. The formal recognition of responsible dissent gave Catholics a greater sense of freedom.

In addition to encouraging greater participation in the liturgy, Vatican II afforded Catholics more opportunities to contribute to decision-making institutions within the Church. Due to a critical shortage of priests in the United States, many parishes do not have an assigned clergyman and are run by lay administrators. At Catholic universities and grade schools lay persons now hold most key administrative positions. And at the national level, American bishops have relied increasingly on lay experts.

American bishops have actively sought advice from the laity when preparing their pastoral letters. The Weakland committee that drafted the bishops' pastoral letter on the economy in 1986 heard testimony from over one hundred individuals, including theologians and biblical scholars, business, labor and political officials, and individuals suffering from the effects of poverty. On a more continual basis, the hierarchy utilizes lay skills through the United States Catholic Conference.

The United States Catholic Conference (USCC), created in 1967, serves as a support for the National Conference of Catholic Bishops. According to the *Official Catholic Directory*:

The USCC is a civil entity of the American Catholic Bishops, incorporated under the laws of the District of Columbia, assisting the Bishops in their service to the Church in this country by uniting the people of God where voluntary collective action on a broad interdiocesan level is needed. The USCC provides an organizational structure and the resources needed to insure coordination, cooperation, and assistance in the public educational, and social concerns of the Church at the national, regional, state and as appropriate diocesan levels.[32]

Made up of lay and religious scholars and policy experts, the USCC plays a major role in developing pastoral letters. In the words of USCC director Ronald Krietemeyer, the decision to staff the USCC with well-trained experts was essential: "To put Vatican II into practice, you needed people with specific knowledge—theologians, but others as well, liturgists, religious educators, fiscal managers, group process specialists. The bishops *needed* technicians to effect renewal."[33] Bishops are not, and cannot be expected to be, experts on all areas of public policy. While most are extremely well educated, their degrees are primarily in the field of religion, not in the social sciences. Bishops must depend upon lay experts if they seek to address complex social and political issues.

While some heralded the call for more lay involvement as the greatest breakthrough from the Council, others argued that the encouragement of greater lay independence, while at the same time reducing the mystique of an all-knowing hierarchy, could exacerbate the spread of "individual religion."[34] Other critics raised a question of credibility.

With major input by lay persons in the preparation of episcopal statements, some are concerned that the credibility of such documents may be undermined. When the hierarchy depends upon the laity for policy guidance and when bishops openly disagree on policy issues, one might wonder what special authority the bishops possess in these areas. The bishops themselves admit that "as bishops, we do not claim to make these prudential judgments with the same kind of authority that marks our declarations of principle."[35] They acknowledge that many of their positions were formulated after an analysis of empirical data that could be open to different interpretations. "Our judgments and recommendations on specific economic issues, therefore, do not carry the same moral authority as our statements of universal moral principles and formal church teaching; the former are related to circumstances which can change or which can be interpreted differently by people of goodwill."[36]

But while the bishops are careful to point out that their specific policy proposals do not carry the full weight of authority, some contend that by issuing such political documents bishops enter a dangerous area that may threaten their authority in other areas. Conservative Philip Lawler contends that "every conscientious Catholic must pay careful attention to the voice of his pastors. But a pastoral letter that delves into such minute political detail cannot be authoritative."[37] By writing in such areas, he maintains, bishops jeopardize their credibility:

Bishops, by virtue of their ordination and consecration, have a special role, and are fortified by the Holy Spirit with a corresponding grace. Thus the bishop is regarded as an authority on theological issues not because of his intellect but because his judgements are guided by the Spirit. . . . The task of applying Catholic teachings to concrete social problems—of devising practical political options—belongs to the laity. When bishops enter into that realm, they not only overextend themselves but also compromise the proper mission of lay people.[38]

To a certain extent, these criticisms reflect political opposition to the bishops. Similar accusations were made against individual bishops who openly confronted laws upholding segregation in the 1960s. They were accused of meddling in politics where they did not belong. Many of the bishops' conservative critics might view the bishops' actions differently if their pastoral letters more forcefully condemned socialism. Many conservatives long for the days of papal encyclicals that condemned the politics of the Left. Nevertheless, if the bishops' statements are regularly ignored, then their leadership could be in serious crisis.

SUPPORT FOR VATICAN II AND BISHOPS' ACTIVISM

While some speculate that many older Catholics may have been disillusioned by changes since the Council, surveys indicate a great deal of support among Catholics for Vatican II. A 1977 Gallup study found that Catholics approve of the reforms of Vatican II by a 67 to 23 percent margin.[39] More specifically, 77 percent of American Catholics support the increase in lay participation in parish decision making.[40] Eighty-four percent agree that the Church should become more ecumenical, seeking "closer relations between Catholics and non-Catholics."[41] In general, most Catholics are happy with the Church. As Gallup and Castelli conclude from their surveys:

The picture of American Catholics that emerges from our data is that of a group of people secure in their sense of identity as Catholics. In some ways, they are extremely upbeat; in other areas, they have some serious criticisms of the Church and some serious disagreements with church teaching. But neither criticisms nor disagreements have changed their sense of belonging to the Church, indeed their sense of ownership of the Church. They believe that their criticisms will eventually be heard, partly because they have institutionalized a sense of change.[42]

The evidence is mixed, however, on Catholic attitudes toward their clergy speaking out on political issues. Steeped in a cultural tradition of church and state separation and Protestant animosity toward religious authority, American Catholics hold mixed feelings about church intervention in politics. Most still view their pastors as religious rather than political leaders. In 1960, Joseph Schuyler found that the most common image of a pastor was that of a "preacher and teacher" rather than a "social leader."[43] Studies conducted in the 1970s continued to show similar results.[44] More recent polls have shown a majority of Catholics opposed to a politically active clergy. Catholics agree 50 to 47 percent with the statement that "priests should not use the pulpit to discuss social issues." They disagree 55 to 39 percent with the statement that "bishops should speak out on political issues like nuclear war and the economy."[45] Hoge and colleagues discovered that younger Catholics are more supportive of social action by the clergy. But since younger Catholics also tend to support more democratic processes within the Church, authoritarian tactics by the bishops may be met with even greater opposition in the future.[46]

When the word "politics" is removed from survey questions, Catholics are more receptive to the idea of their bishops speaking out on the morality of social issues. The pro-choice group, Catholics for a Free Choice, conducted a survey in which they asked the question, "Do you think the Catholic bishops should use the political arena to advance their moral opinion?" Seventy-one percent of Catholics and 78 percent of non-Catholics answered "no." The organization concluded from this that "the results of this poll clearly show that both Catholic and non-Catholics have profound misgivings about the involvement of the Catholic bishops in political issues."[47] In a more recent poll announced by the United States bishops' conference, bishops countered the poll by Catholics for a Free Choice. Their poll found that 69 percent agreed that religious leaders who opposed abortion have the right to "advocate [their] position to the public, including elected officials."[48] The bishops' poll avoided the use of the words "politics" or "political."

Negative connotations associated with the word "politics" turn many people off. In the present study many bishops conveyed a similar aversion to the term. Several expressed concern with the use of the word in our survey. Few want to acknowledge that their actions may be "political." Expressing frustration over the mixed public reaction to their activities, one American bishop stated, "Vatican II carried on social teaching based on the Gospel and emphasized by Leo XIII. The U.S. Bishops have tried to implement it in the spirit of our American democratic tradition and principles, often at the cost of misunderstanding. The Church's teaching and practice are not political, per se." Another bishop attributes Catholics' "impoverished understanding of the role of the contemporary social teaching of the Church in their own lives [to] an unnuanced prejudice on the part of many [that] 'the Church should stay out of politics.' " Future studies of religion and politics, especially those utilizing surveys, ought to attempt to define more clearly (or allow respondents to define for themselves) the meaning of the word "politics."

In addition to an aversion to direct "political" intervention, Catholics also resent episcopal interference in the area of sexual morality. It is in the area of sexual morality that Catholics maintain clear disagreements with their Church. Despite consistently taught church opposition, only 33 percent of American Catholics believe that premarital sex is wrong, while 73 percent believe Catholics should be allowed to practice artificial means of birth control.[49] When it comes to abortion, only about one in four Catholics subscribes to the official church teaching that abortion should be illegal under all circumstances.[50] As Gallup and Castelli conclude, "The simple fact is that the Catholic Church has not merely lost its credibility on birth control—it has lost much of its credibility on everything related to sex. . . . When it comes to sex, church leaders are preaching to an audience that is simply not paying any attention."[51]

On other issues, however, Catholics are more receptive to church teaching. From his study of Catholic parishioners, David Leege concludes that

when church leaders exercise their teaching authority on political or social questions, they will often receive a polite reception from American Catholic parishioners. Nevertheless, the closer the teaching gets to personal morality, the less authority the people accord to it. . . . Except for perhaps a quarter of the parishioners who routinely consider church teaching highly suspect, the pronouncements of church leaders may help shape the dialogue along with other political forces.[52]

In actuality, then, Catholics may be more receptive to their bishops than some polls suggest. The extent to which the laity supports the social action of the hierarchy is mixed and is dependent on the nature of that involvement. Overtly political actions to affect elections or silence politicians may backfire on bishops. The laity turns off to authoritarian tactics. With the spirit of Vatican II as a guide, they demand a voice in the Church. Most do not reject bishops offering moral guidance on political issues as with the peace and economic pastoral letters. But they want to be consulted.

POLITICAL MOBILIZATION AND THE CHURCH COMMUNITY

While American evangelical and fundamentalist Protestant leaders in the 1980s engaged in intense efforts to mobilize new voters and recruit political candidates for the political Right,[53] Roman Catholics were also called by their bishops to actively participate in politics. With inspiration from the Second Vatican Council, Catholic leaders sought to raise the political consciousness of their followers. In 1979 bishops openly encouraged Catholics "to become involved in the campaign or party of your choice."[54] They endorsed the development of political study groups where Catholics could come together to learn the Church's social teachings. Forty-two percent of bishops responding to our survey say they have actually organized such a group in their diocese.

Other institutions encouraged by the Council offer additional opportunities for political learning. The laity are assuming new leadership roles within the Church.[55] Parish councils comprised of parishioners elected by their peers offer Catholics experience in governmental procedures. New programs including political study groups, Renew, and RCIA (Rite of Christian Initiation of Adults) offer opportunities for social networking and a place to learn the social teachings of the Church. The Renew program consists of sessions in which church members assemble in small groups to discuss the personal and social dimensions of their faith. The RCIA program brings prospective Catholics seeking baptism and/or confirmation together with personal sponsors to learn the Catholic faith. This weekly program, which runs from the fall to late spring, offers a strong emphasis on post–Vatican II social teaching.

As the Second Vatican Council's call for increased lay involvement is realized, new opportunities for increased political mobilization may be possible. In fact, Gallup found that, while church attendance has declined, participation in other religious activities has risen over the last ten years.[56] The Catholic parish has become an outlet for social action. "Today's Catholics turn to their parish as participants and leaders, using it as an outlet for their talents. The parish is no longer a haven from the outside community, it is a vehicle for relating to and transforming that community."[57]

As with the nature of the bishops' political activism, the issue of lay participation in the Church has divided liberals and conservatives within the Catholic Church. Conservatives worry that too much lay participation may infringe upon the domain of the priest. Pope John Paul II has expressed concern over the "tendency toward a 'clericalization' of the lay faithful." Warning pastors to exercise "maximum care" when assigning lay persons to church duties, the pontiff is concerned about "a too indiscriminate use of the word 'ministry.' "[58]

Catholic parishioners active in parish councils and liturgical and educational programs are more likely to be involved also in civic activities outside the parish. Those involved in social welfare and social justice groups are among the most politically active outside of the church.[59] Studies of post–Vatican II innovations in church programs suggest that where these programs exist, political differences are evident. Andrew Musetto contrasts the new "experimental" parishes with traditional parishes. The innovative institutions more closely follow the spirit of Vatican II (though they are not always sanctioned by the Church). Parishioners in these parishes tend to be more liberal in their outlook than are their more traditional counterparts.[60]

A study of the implementation of the bishops' Campaign for Human Development suggests that when a program is vigorously pushed by leaders within the Church, parishioners will respond. The socially progressive Campaign for Human Development, created by the bishops in 1969, seeks to carry out the Vatican II call to assist the poor and oppressed throughout the world. The more a parish gets involved in this program, the more support for this type of action is generated.[61] Davidson and colleagues found that support tends to follow church attempts to increase involvement in social concerns.[62] Their findings generally support the conclusion that "behavior change typically precedes, rather than follows from, attitude change."[63]

Such findings would seem to be good news for Catholic leaders who seek to influence the political attitudes of their followers. One would expect that the longer post–Vatican II programs are in effect, the greater the number of Catholics who will come around to the views of the Council. Movement of Catholic attitudes toward those of their bishops might be accelerated with further implementation of programs inspired by Vatican II.

CATHOLIC POLITICAL ATTITUDES

Church-affiliated Catholics might be expected to be more closely in tune with their bishops since they have more exposure to official church teaching. Yet, like their bishops, lay Catholics are not in agreement on political issues. And they show both similarities and dissimilarities with their bishops.

To compare American Catholics with their bishops, the following section uses survey results from national polls conducted by the Gallup organization, results of surveys of parish-connected Catholics conducted by the Notre Dame Study of Catholic Parish Life, and results of our own survey of the bishops.

Prior studies seeking to compare Catholics and their bishops have related Catholic political attitudes with official positions taken by the bishops in formal pastoral letters and statements. In a study conducted in this vein, Gallup and Castelli concluded that "American Catholics are in substantial agreement with the bishops on broad economic themes: a strong role for the government in economic matters, the role of circumstances in forcing people into poverty, the need for tax reform and the redistribution of wealth and income in more equitable fashion."[64]

Not all bishops, however, support the formal pastoral statements. Therefore, survey results of bishops' attitudes offer a more nuanced comparison of political positions.

PARTISAN PREFERENCE

Many studies have demonstrated the political differences between Catholics and Protestants in the United States. While mainline Protestants have tended toward conservative politics and the Republican party, American Catholics have historically maintained close ties with the Democratic party.[65] Particularly with the Democratic nominations of Catholic presidential candidates Al Smith and John Kennedy, Catholics have been a major core group of the Democratic party coalition.[66] As the Democratic party welcomed Catholic immigrants coming from Europe at the turn of the century, the party served as a refuge from nativist hostilities. With the New Deal programs of Franklin Roosevelt, Catholics found hope for economic improvement.

Those who attribute Catholic attachment to the Democrats to the historically lower economic and social status of Catholics speculate that as Catholics move up in socioeconomic status, they will move further to the Right and toward the Republican party.[67] Better than twenty years ago Catholics had already achieved economic parity with Protestants.[68] By the 1980s, however, Catholics were still more likely than Protestants to be Democratic at all income and education levels.[69] The roots of Catholic politics go deeper than economics.

Debate continues over the question of whether an individual's religious beliefs and practices or class is the more important determinant of party preference. While Berelson and Steiner maintain that "class is the single most important differentiator of political preferences across societies,"[70] others question the extent of class influence. Philip Converse argues that social differences, including religious cleavages, may have "greater penetration into mass publics than do class differences, as far as consequences for political behavior are concerned."[71] He maintains that religion is in "the front rank of determinants" of partisan preference. "The general rule seems to be that religious differentiation intrudes on partisan political alignments in [an] unexpectedly powerful degree wherever it conceivably can."[72]

In a study on social cohesion, political parties, and strains in regimes in seventeen Western countries, Rose and Urwin find that religion (as measured by confessional affiliation, church attendance, and pro- and anti-clerical opinion) provides a stronger basis for cohesiveness in political parties than any other variable, including class. The authors conclude that "religious divisions, not class, are the main social basis of parties in the Western world today."[73] In my own cross-national study of partisan preference patterns in Europe during the late 1970s, I found religion to be strongly correlated with party attachments in most countries. The religious influence, however, is conditioned by cultural contexts. "Whereas Catholicism is a force of conservatism among frequent church attenders in some countries (France, Germany and Italy)," I argue, "it is not in others (Britain and the Netherlands). In countries where Protestantism is the dominant religion (Britain and Denmark), Protestantism is a force of conservatism."[74] The cultural and theological distinctions between religions are, in part, responsible for political differences and may explain tendencies toward specific political orientations.

Despite close ties to the Democratic party, American Catholics have in the past shown a penchant for conservative politics. Those predicting Republican gains among Catholics point to the more conservative attitudes among working class Catholics on issues of national defense and social morality. This conservative strain within Catholicism has been attributed to the influence of religious leaders and Catholic religious theology. The social conservativism and hawkish foreign policy stands of many Catholics was reflected in the outspokenness of prominent conservative Catholic leaders including Cardinal Francis Spellman, Father Charles E. Coughlin, and Senator Joseph McCarthy.[75] A Catholic theology that for a long time stressed the importance of the afterlife rather than the immediate human condition has been blamed as a barrier to economic and social reform. As a socialist in early twentieth-century Great Britain lamented, this "otherworldly" view was an impediment to progressive social reform:

Table 6.1
Partisan Identification of Catholics and Bishops (Percentages)

	All Catholics[1]	Church attenders[2] (n = 2667)	Bishops
Republican	20%	19%	23%
Democrat	44	48	52
Independent/ No preference	36	33	25

1. *Source:* 1980–1985 pooled National Opinion Research Center General Social Surveys. Reported in Michael Corbett, *American Public Opinion* (New York: Longman, 1991), p. 246.
2. *Source:* Data from survey of 2,667 registered Catholic parishioners included in the Notre Dame Study of Catholic Parish Life. Reported in David C. Leege, "Catholics and the Civic Order: Parish Participation, Politics, and Civic Participation," *Review of Politics* 50, no. 4 (Fall 1988), pp. 704–736.

Rome never forgot the individual and was sensitive to every change in his condition or prospects. But she took little account of this perishing life, and her regard for the human body was very much that of the medieval ascetic or Jesuit priest. The soul alone persists and endures. The salvation of the soul is, then, the great end of life and all saviours. Nothing else matters. The people's children suffered and had suffered more cruelly during this century and the last, than ever before. No matter. The stake and the rack have a place in the scheme of salvation. The insanitary area may also cure heretics, may discipline fruitfully even the children of Mother Church.[76]

Since the Second Vatican Council, however, things have changed greatly. With the exception of their outspokenness against abortion, American bishops are markedly liberal in their political outlook. The Church teaches that an obligation to improve the human condition is integrally tied to salvation. To the extent that the Democratic party is more supportive than the Republican party of governmental programs to address social and economic inequality, an affiliation of Catholics with such a party would signify an ideological consistency.

Many studies have substantiated the association between Catholics and the Democratic party.[77] This association is even stronger among Catholic bishops, who are more versed in the tradition of Catholic social teaching. As indicated in Table 6.1, American bishops are four percentage points more likely to identify as Democrats than are Catholic churchgoers and eight percentage points more likely than all Catholics to identify with the Democratic party. Consistent with theories suggesting greater partisanship among the politically sophisticated, bishops are more likely than lay Catholics to state partisan preference. Only 25 percent of bishops (compared to 33 percent of frequent church attenders and 36 percent of all Catholics) identify as nonpartisans or independents.

These findings, which show parish-connected Catholics to be more like their bishops when it comes to party affiliation, tend to refute Lenski's theory that those most closely allied with religion tend toward political conservatism and the Republican party.[78] To the extent that the politically progressive message of Vatican II is emphasized by American bishops, church-affiliated Catholics may be expected to move closer to their bishops and further to the political Left. Closer affiliation with a church that emphasizes a theology of social action to combat inequality can lead to a more liberal political outlook and greater attachment to the Democratic party. Earlier studies that emphasized the tendency toward conservativism among frequent church attenders relied on data collected during the 1950s and early 1960s (a time of greater conservatism within Catholicism), before the introduction of major changes within the Catholic Church.

On more specific issues of public policy, church-affiliated Catholics are also closer to their bishops and the more liberal positions bishops espouse (see Table 6.2). Church-affiliated Catholics are somewhat closer to their bishops than Catholics in general on attitudes toward the death penalty, busing to achieve racial integration, and gun control. They are most supportive of a bilateral nuclear freeze. Given that they are more likely to hear these issues discussed in their parish community, greater similarity with the bishops is not surprising. Andrew Greeley correlates the increased Catholic support for a nuclear freeze with the extensive media coverage given the bishops' pastoral letter "Challenge of Peace."[79]

In the area of homosexual rights, however, frequent church attenders are least supportive of equality. On an issue that they may view as a question of sexual morality rather than a person's civil rights, church affiliated Catholics are least willing to allow homosexuals to teach in the public schools, while the bishops are most supportive of homosexual rights. It may be that as Catholic church attenders are more likely to accept the Church's teaching on sexual morality, they may be influenced by the

Table 6.2
Percentage of Catholics and Bishops Favoring Various Government Policies

	All Catholics[1]	Church attenders[2] (n = 2667)	Bishops
Death penalty for persons convicted of murder	75	65	19
The Equal Rights Amendment (ERA)	69	69	42
Requiring prayer in public schools	72	69	69
Allowing homosexuals to teach in public schools	41	35	56
Ban on handguns	49	74*	92
Busing to achieve racial integration in public schools	20	26	64
Nuclear weapons freeze	84	92	79
Tuition tax credits	--	83	98
Increased spending on social programs	77	--	89

1. *Source:* George Gallup, Jr., and Jim Castelli, *The American Catholic People: Their Beliefs, Practices, and Values* (Garden City, N.Y.: Doubleday, 1987).
2. *Source:* Data from survey of 2,667 registered Catholic parishioners included in the Notre Dame Study of Catholic Parish Life. Reported in David C. Leege, "Catholics and the Civic Order: Parish Participation, Politics, and Civic Participation," *Review of Politics* 50, no. 4 (Fall 1988), pp. 704–736.
*The gun control question in the Notre Dame study is different from that asked of all Catholics and the bishops. Catholic church attenders were asked whether they supported "registration of all firearms." This makes a direct comparison somewhat problematic.

church ban on the practice of homosexuality when they express their opposition to allowing homosexuals to teach in the schools. They may not view this as a civil rights issue, as many bishops do.

Nevertheless, on most other issues, Catholics who attend church regularly are closer to their bishops' political views than are Catholics in general.

CONCLUSION

It would seem that the official church social teaching and the teaching of American bishops does trickle down to the parish level. Catholics by large margins support the reforms of Vatican II and are generally receptive to the political activism of their bishops, so long as that action remains nonpartisan. If this is the case, the message of Vatican II can be expected to continue to influence American Catholics and may work to move Catholics toward more liberal politics.

To the extent that conservative leaders within the Church seek to slow the reforms of Vatican II and return to more authoritarian practices, however, the implementation of Vatican II may be slowed.[80] But most signs continue to indicate a Catholic backlash to such efforts, particularly when the authoritarian tactics are used in the area of sexual ethics and abortion. It is in these areas that Catholics are least receptive to church authority. Nevertheless, the more progressive political and economic message of Vatican II and American bishops is getting through.

The bishops are faced with a dilemma. Do they emphasize issues where they have greater influence, or do they push an unpopular agenda and risk being ignored by their followers?

NOTES

1. Bryan Wilson, *Religion in Sociological Perspective* (Oxford, England: Oxford University Press, 1982), p. 170.

2. Peter L. Berger, *The Sacred Canopy: Elements of a Sociological Theory of Religion* (Garden City, N.Y.: Doubleday, 1967), p. 127.

3. Wilson, *Religion in Sociological Perspective*, p. 168.

4. Michael Novak, *The Open Church* (New York: Macmillan, 1964), and James Hitchcock, *The Decline and Fall of Radical Catholicism* (New York: Herder and Herder, 1971).

5. William D. Dinges, "Ritual Conflict as Social Conflict: Liturgical Reform in the Roman Catholic Church," *Sociological Analysis* 48, no. 2 (Summer 1987), pp. 138–157.

6. See "Church Attendance Stable, Poll Shows," *San Francisco Chronicle*, December 19, 1988.

7. George Gallup, Jr., and Jim Castelli, *The American Catholic People: Their Beliefs, Practices, and Values* (Garden City, N.Y.: Doubleday, 1987), p. 12.

8. "Church Attendance Stable."

9. See Andrew M. Greeley, "Council or Encyclical," *Review of Religious Research* 18, no. 1 (Fall 1976), p. 3, and Andrew M. Greeley and Michael Hout, "The Center Doesn't Hold: Church Attendance in the United States, 1940–1984, *American Sociological Review* 52, no. 3 (June 1987), pp. 325–345.

10. Gallup and Castelli, *The American Catholic People*, p. 173.

11. Ibid., p. 28.

12. Stephen Harding and David Phillips with Michael Fogarty, *Contrasting Values in Western Europe* (London: Macmillan, 1986), p. 69.

13. This is evident among Americans as well. See Robert N. Bellah, Richard Madsen, William M. Sullivan, Ann Swidler, and Steven M. Tipton, *Habits of the Heart* (New York: Harper and Row, 1985).

14. Wade Clark Roof, "Concepts and Indicators of Religious Commitment: A Critical Review," in Robert Wuthnow, ed., *The Religious Dimension: New Directions in Quantitative Research* (New York: Academic Press, 1979), p. 31.

15. Thomas Luckmann, *The Invisible Religion* (New York: Macmillan, 1967), p. 116.

16. Ibid., p. 86.

17. As the priest shortage in the United States becomes increasingly critical today, the Church may be forced again to rely, more so than she might prefer, on the services of lay Catholics. While nonordained Catholics are not permitted to celebrate (consecrate) the Mass, many are asked to lead replacement liturgical services in parishes without priests. Many parishes without priests have lay "pastors" assigned instead.

18. Daniel Callahan, *The Mind of the Catholic Layman* (New York: Scribner's, 1963), p. 17.

19. John Tracy Ellis, *American Catholicism*, 2nd ed. (Chicago: University of Chicago Press, 1969), p. 46.

20. Callahan, *The Mind of the Catholic Layman*, p. 24.

21. Quoted in ibid., p. 25.

22. Ibid., p. 23.

23. For a discussion of the role of the laity prior to Vatican II, see Jean Guitton, *The Church and the Laity: From Newman to Vatican II* (Staten Island, N.Y.: Alba House, 1965).

24. Quoted in Alberic Stacpoole, ed., *Vatican II Revisited by Those who Were There* (London: Geoffrey Chapman, 1986), p. 2.

25. See Ludwig Eisenhofer, *The Liturgy of the Roman Rite* (New York: Herder and Herder, 1953), p. 3.

26. See, for example, Dietrich Von Hildebrand, *The Devastated Vineyard* (Chicago: Franciscan Herald Press, 1973), p. 250.

27. For a good review of the literature see Dinges, "Ritual Conflict as Social Conflict."

28. See Robert L. Johnstone, "Public Images of Protestant Ministers and Catholic Priests: An Empirical Study of Anti-Clericalism in the U.S.," *Sociological Analysis* 33, no. 1 (Spring 1972), pp. 34–49; Andrew M. Greeley, *The American Catholic: A Social Portrait* (New York: Basic Books, 1977) and Dean Hoge et al., *Research on Men's Vocations to the Priesthood and Religious Life* (Washington, D.C.: United States Catholic Conference Office of Research, 1984).

29. Dinges, "Ritual Conflict as Social Conflict," p. 148.

30. Vatican Council II, *Gaudium et spes*, in Austin P. Flannery, ed., *Documents of Vatican II* (Grand Rapids, Mich.: Eerdmans, 1975), p. 944, par. 43.

31. Ibid., p. 968, par. 62.

32. C. Jeanne Hanline, ed., *Official Catholic Directory* (Wilmette, Ill.: Kenedy and Sons, 1988), p. xxviii.

33. Quoted in Mary Hanna, "Bishops as Political Leaders," in Charles W. Dunn, ed., *Religion in American Politics* (Washington, D.C.: CQ Press, 1989), p. 78.

34. See Michael F. Aliosi, "Vatican II, Ecumenism and a Parsonian Analysis of Change," *Sociological Analysis* 49, no. 1 (Spring 1988), pp. 25–26.

35. National Conference of Catholic Bishops, "Economic Justice for All: Pastoral Letter on Catholic Social Teaching and the U.S. Economy," in Hugh J. Nolan, ed., *Pastoral Letters of the United States Catholic Bishops,* vol. 5, 1983–1988 (Washington, D.C.: United States Catholic Conference, 1989), p. 375.

36. Ibid., p. 420.

37. Philip Lawler, *How Bishops Decide* (Washington, D.C.: Ethics and Public Policy Center, 1986), p. 35.

38. Ibid., pp. 37–38.

39. Reported in Gallup and Castelli, *The American Catholic People*, p. 49.

40. Ibid., p. 56.

41. Ibid., p. 49.

42. Ibid., p. 43.

43. Joseph B. Schuyler, *Northern Parish* (Chicago: Loyola University Press, 1960).

44. See examples in Robert Dixon and Dean Hoge, "Models and Priorities of the Catholic Church as Held by Suburban Laity," *Review of Religious Research* 20, no. 2 (Spring 1979), pp. 150–167.

45. Jim Castelli, "A Tale of Two Cultures," *Notre Dame Magazine* 15 (Summer 1987), pp. 33–34.

46. Hoge et al., *Research on Men's Vocations to the Priesthood.*

47. KRC Research and Consulting, Inc., "Summary of Findings: National Poll on the Catholic Church and Abortion," prepared for Catholics for a Free Choice, #2640, October 1990.

48. Cited in *National Catholic Reporter*, February 22, 1991, p. 4.

49. Gallup and Castelli, *The American Catholic People*, pp. 51–52.

50. Ibid., p. 95.

51. Ibid., p. 183.

52. David C. Leege, "Catholics and the Civic Order: Parish Participation, Politics, and Civic Participation," *The Review of Politics* 50, no. 4 (Fall 1988), p. 733.

53. See, for example, Erling Jorstad, *The Politics of Moralism: The New Christian Right in American Life* (Minneapolis: Augsburg 1981), and Stephen D. Johnson and Joseph B. Tamney, eds., *The Political Role of Religion in the United States* (Boulder, Colo.: Westview Press, 1986).

54. Administrative Board of the United States Catholic Conference, "Political Responsibility: Choices for the 1980s," October 26, 1979, in Nolan, *Pastoral Letters*, vol. 4, p. 319.

55. See James D. Whitehead and Evelyn Eaton Whitehead, *The Emerging Laity: Returning Leadership to the Community of Faith* (Garden City, N.Y.: Doubleday, 1986).

56. Gallup and Castelli, *The American Catholic People*, p. 30.

57. Jim Castelli and Joseph Gremillion, *The Emerging Parish: The Notre Dame Study of Catholic Life since Vatican II* (San Francisco: Harper and Row, 1987).

58. See "Pope Warns Churches on Use of Laity," *San Francisco Chronicle*, January 31, 1989.

59. See David C. Leege, "Catholics and the Civic Order." Walter Broughton found that among Protestants, those who attend church meetings are more likely to see the church as having an active role in society. See Walter Broughton, "Religiosity and Opposition to Church Social Action: A Test for a Weberian Hypothesis," *Review of Religious Research* 19, no. 2 (Winter 1978), pp. 154–166.

60. Andrew P. Musetto, "Innovators in the Catholic Church," *Review of Religious Research* 17, no. 1 (Fall 1975), pp. 28–36.

61. Bernard Evans, "Campaign for Human Development: Church Involvement in Social Change," *Review of Religious Research* 20, no. 3 (Summer 1979), pp. 264–278.

62. James D. Davidson, Ronald Elly, Thomas Hull, and Donald Nead, "Increasing Church Involvement in Social Concerns: A Model for Human Ministries," *Review of Religious Research* 20, no. 3 (Summer 1979), pp. 291–314.

63. Ibid., p. 295.

64. Gallup and Castelli, *The American Catholic People*, p. 67.

65. Paul F. Lazarsfeld, Bernard Berelson, and Hazel Gaudet, *The People's Choice: How the Voter Makes Up His Mind in a Presidential Campaign* (New York: Columbia University Press, 1948); Bernard Berelson, Paul F. Lazarsfeld, and William N. McPhee, *Voting: A Study of Opinion Formation in a Presidential Campaign* (Chicago: University of Chicago Press, 1954); Gerhard Lenski, *The Religious Factor* (Garden City, N.Y.: Doubleday–Anchor, 1963).

66. Philip E. Converse, "Religion and Politics: The 1960 Election," in Angus Campbell et al., eds., *Elections and the Political Order* (New York: Wiley, 1966), pp. 96–124; John H. Fenton, *The Catholic Vote* (New Orleans: Hauser

Press, 1960); Andrew M. Greeley, "How Conservative Are American Catholics?" *Political Science Quarterly* 92, no. 2 (Summer 1977), pp. 199–218.

67. Kevin Phillips, *The Emerging Republican Majority* (New York: Doubleday–Anchor, 1969); John H. Whyte, *Catholics in Western Democracies: A Study in Political Behavior* (New York: St. Martin's Press, 1981); Scott Greer, "Catholic Voters and the Democratic Party," *Public Opinion Quarterly* 25, no. 4 (Winter 1961), pp. 611–625; E. J. Dionne, Jr., "Catholics and the Democrats: Estrangement but Not Desertion," in Seymour M. Lipset, ed., *Party Coalitions in the 1980s* (San Francisco: Institute for Contemporary Studies, 1981), pp. 307–325.

68. Andrew M. Greeley, *The American Catholic: A Social Portrait* (New York: Basic Books, 1977), p. 20.

69. Michael Corbett, *American Public Opinion: Trends, Processes, and Patterns* (New York: Longman, 1991), p. 247.

70. Bernard Berelson and Gary A. Steiner, *Human Behavior: An Inventory of Scientific Findings* (New York: Harcourt, Brace and World, 1964), p. 427.

71. Philip E. Converse, "The Nature of Belief Systems in Mass Publics," in David E. Apter, ed., *Ideology and Discontent* (New York: Free Press, 1964), pp. 247–248.

72. Philip E. Converse, "Some Priority Variables in Comparative Electoral Research," in Richard Rose, ed., *Electoral Behavior: A Comparative Handbook* (New York: Free Press, 1974), p. 734.

73. Richard Rose and D. Urwin, "Social Cohesion, Political Parties and Strains in Regimes," *Comparative Political Studies* 2, no. 1 (April 1969), p. 12.

74. Richard J. Gelm, "Religion and Partisan Preference in Europe" (Paper presented at the 1989 Annual Meeting of the American Political Science Association, Atlanta, Georgia), p. 20.

75. Seymour Martin Lipset, "Three Decades of the Radical Right: Coughlinites, McCarthyites, and Birchers," in Daniel Bell, ed., *The Radical Right* (Garden City, N.Y.: Doubleday–Anchor, 1964), pp. 373–446; David F. Crosby, *God, Church, and Flag: Senator Joseph R. McCarthy and the Catholic Church, 1950–1957* (Chapel Hill: University of North Carolina Press, 1978). For a biography of the hawkish Cardinal Francis Spellman, see John Cooney, *The American Pope* (New York: Times Books, 1984).

76. Margaret McMillan, *The Life of Rachel McMillan* (London: J. M. Dent, 1927), p. 88.

77. See, for example, Greeley, "How Conservative Are American Catholics?" pp. 199–218; Joan L. Fee, "Political Continuity and Change," in Andrew M. Greeley et al., *Catholic Schools in a Declining Church* (Kansas City: Sheed and Ward, 1976), and Gallup and Castelli, *The American Catholic People.*

78. Lenski, *The Religious Factor.*

79. See Andrew M. Greeley, *American Catholics since the Council: An Unauthorized Report* (Chicago: Thomas More Press, 1985).

80. One such conservative facing a public backlash is Bishop John J. Meyers of Peoria, Illinois. See Robert McClory, "Catholic Bishop's Ultra-Orthodoxy May Not Play in Peoria," *National Catholic Reporter*, May 24, 1991, p. 6.

Chapter 7 _____

Conclusion: The Enduring Connection Between Religion and Politics

While many point to the decline of religion in modern political systems, this study has addressed the continuing importance of religion in shaping the process of political development, nurturing political cultures, and influencing the political values of American Catholics. Despite a common perception that the tie between religion and politics has been severed, the connection between these two realms is complex and persistent, though it has undergone change. While the role of religion is no longer as dominant as that in traditional societies, it nonetheless remains a salient force in modern systems.

A dynamic view of religion and its capacity for change is needed to fully appreciate the complexity of the religious influence. The main emphasis of early Christian theology was on the importance of the community of believers. Since early Christians suffered from discrimination and persecution, the Church became a defender of the outcast and downtrodden. As the Church was accepted by and absorbed into the state in the fourth century, church fathers preached the virtues of obedience and submission to the state. Especially since Vatican II, however, as the Catholic Church has sought to reconcile its position within the modern world, it has attempted to return to its earlier roots and has been more willing to side with the poor and oppressed. An emphasis has been placed on reforming the world's economic and political systems in order to secure the human rights of all persons, especially the poor. A Catholicism that once stressed obedience and submission to temporal powers has now found a justification for siding with the underclasses. The emphasis on a preferential option for the poor marks a significant shift away from a church aligned with the powerful.

Though Catholicism in the past tended toward conservatism, seeking the maintenance of the political status quo, the Catholic Church now must be viewed as more progressive. Many of the tenets of democracy challenged by Catholicism during the eighteenth and nineteenth centuries were embraced by the Church at the Second Vatican Council. More recently, rather than defending the status quo against the forces of democracy in the Philippines, Central America, and Eastern Europe, the Church has played a leading role in fighting for democratic change. It has become more tolerant of other faiths, preaching the virtues of ecumenism.

Changes occurring within Christianity throughout its 2,000-year history have reverberated throughout society as religion has impacted political development and political cultures. Religion and politics are intertwined, sometimes in a symbiotic relationship. Religion often provides a legitimacy for the state, but religion also makes demands on the political system. While religion is often of ultimate concern to the individual, the state is often looked upon to help realize religious objectives. When change occurs in one realm, its impact is felt in the other.

The great break within Christianity occurring during the Protestant Reformation illustrates the tremendous capacity for transformations within religion. The Reformation was marked by the formulations of Christian theologies more conducive to political changes occurring in Europe. But in a reciprocal way, Protestantism would also be affected by politics. While early Protestant theology offered legitimacy to the forces of radical change, Protestantism would become a force of conservatism when it was absorbed into the state.

Within Catholicism change would also come. Despite the Church's initial resistance, Catholicism had the long-forgotten biblical notion of God working through historical change to allow it to proceed as it did with Vatican II. In essence, the Protestant Reformation and the Second Vatican Council were attempts to get back to the bases of earlier Christian teachings, and they illustrate the capacity for religious reformulations within Christianity.

Historically, the Roman Catholic Church has made significant contributions to the political development of the Western world. During the Middle Ages, the Church provided a centralized authority around which Europe could grow. After the Reformation, the proliferation of Christian sects and secular challenges to religion compelled religious leaders to mobilize believers through political parties, so as to maintain an influence in society. No longer able to directly influence the state and limited in its control over its own followers, the Church was compelled to adapt.

The Second Vatican Council was a formal recognition by Catholic leaders that the Church no longer held the position of influence to which it had grown accustomed during the Middle Ages. For centuries after its power was in decline in Europe, the Church fought to maintain control, often by way of authoritarian and repressive sanctions. Many church leaders did not want to relinquish (or accept the inevitable loss of) power. By the middle of the twentieth century, however, as democracy was firmly established in Europe, authoritarian tactics became increasingly out-moded. The Church sought better ways to make its message persuasive. Dialogue and open inquiry were encouraged to better formulate and disseminate Catholic social teaching and to provide more effective ways for religion to influence political values.

How the Church can affect political culture or political values, however, has been a question of much debate. In the United States, the Catholic influence on American political culture has been limited. Dominated for most of America's history by a Protestant majority hostile to Catholics, Catholic leaders maintained a low profile. But that has changed. American Catholic bishops have now assumed a leadership position as spokespersons on American political culture.

Changes emanating from the Second Vatican Council are most responsible for the episcopal shift. The social message of Catholicism, articulated by bishops at the Second Vatican Council, has been primarily responsible for the increased political activism of America's bishops. Catholic theology and complex social teaching have not been readily available to the laity. Vatican II sought to change this by encouraging dialogue and cooperation in developing and implementing Catholic social teaching. A theology that once stressed the importance of preparing for the afterlife to the neglect of the temporal world now emphasizes a social responsibility to improve social, economic, and political conditions in the world.

As religious theology changes, so also do opportunities for changes in the behavior of religious followers. This has been obvious at the level of American Catholic bishops. They quickly responded to the Second Vatican Council's call by establishing the National Conference of Catholic Bishops in 1966 and aggressively working on pastoral letters, including "Challenge of Peace" and "Economic Justice for All." Closely connected and obedient to the Church and very familiar with its teaching, American bishops were readily responsive to Vatican II. For most American Catholics not versed in Catholic social teaching, however, change came and was absorbed more slowly. As different religious emphases are pushed by church hierarchs, these changes must work their way through the cultural system.

Doctrinal and theological change cannot by themselves account for the varieties of religious influence on politics. Those changes must filter through a complex social system until they reach the average citizen. David Laitin has pointed out at least three points of religious influence on politics.[1] At one level is the doctrinal discernment of theologians. Known by only a few experts and church authorities, these teachings are not readily available to the ordinary Catholic. Catholic popes issued major encyclicals on the modern social teaching of the Church for a hundred years, beginning with Pope Leo XIII's *Rerum novarum*. Yet few Catholics have any cognizance of these publications. The religious doctrine must be filtered through the complex system of ideas emanating from a variety of sources. At this second level, there exists a "practical religion" which "emerges out of the interaction of doctrine and social origins of the ideas."[2] This practical religion often differs from the original intent of the doctrine, and is continually modified to meet the changing social conditions within the system. The Church continually grapples with the task of clarifying its teaching and maintaining its relevance in a changing world. The Second Vatican Council illustrates an impetus for change, but since the Council the Church still strives to adapt. Conservatives and liberals within the Church continue to argue over the "real meaning" of Vatican II. At a third level religious influence stems from the way in which a community of converts may adapt the doctrine to meet their own cultural conditions. American bishops must work with an American Catholic community covetous of its independence and anxious for greater reform within the Church. Catholics are generally receptive to the bishops' dialogue on political and economic questions, yet they reject episcopal actions seen as directly political or authoritarian. Many Catholics have embraced Pope John XXIII's call for the "use of the medicine of mercy rather than that of severity."[3] They seek a more compassionate church. Bishops seeking obedience from their followers must confront the effects of changes that pull Catholics toward greater freedom and independence in their beliefs and practices.

Trying to balance tradition with change often pits traditionalists against progressives. Many church leaders are concerned by what they see as an overly permissive mentality on the part of American Catholics. Church leaders in Rome are worried about the direction of the American Catholic Church. The conservative reaction of some bishops and the present pope is hardly without precedent. History is replete with leaders who, seeking to stem the loss of their power, tighten discipline and attempt to stifle dissent. With any changes, particularly those so profound as the reforms of Vatican II, there is likely to be a tension between those seeking the maintenance of the status quo and those supportive of reform. How to find a balance between the forces of continuity and change, however, is a far from simple process.

Sanctions against progressive American bishops Raymond Hunthausen of Seattle and Rembert Weakland of Milwaukee signify a contest over the direction of the American Church and the political direction of the bishops' episcopal conference. Recent appointments to the American hierarchy illustrate the attempt by Rome to appoint bishops more allegiant to official church dogma and the views of the current pope. Pope John Paul II has appointed bishops more politically conservative than bishops appointed by Popes John XXIII and Paul VI.

A person's religious views are often reflected in similar orientations to politics. An orientation emanating from the Second Vatican Council stressing collegial authority, dialogue with the laity, ecumenism, and efforts to improve the temporal world are conducive to a political orientation on the political left. While John Paul II's bishops are more likely to be Republicans and self-described political conservatives, they are also less likely to support efforts to go even further with implementing the social and political teachings of Vatican II. While most every bishop expresses support for the teachings of the Council, there is a rift between church leaders on questions concerning the extent to push for reform and which particular aspects of the Council teaching deserve greatest attention.

Despite the tensions, however, the Church has been relatively effective in implementing reforms of the Council. Most American Catholics (including bishops) do not want to return to pre–Vatican II methods. The Church has made significant inroads in implementing Vatican II reforms, particularly in the area of the Mass. This has worked to demystify the ceremony, and with it the position of the priest. Now seen as fallible, average human beings, priests are no longer as likely to command the obedience from parishioners that in the past might have been more forthcoming.

American Catholics heartily embrace Vatican II reforms to elevate the status of lay Catholics. They anticipate even greater opportunities for lay participation in the important decisions of the Church. To the extent that participation has already increased, it has worked to encourage Catholics to become more active in the outer social and political environment. The parish community is now a learning workshop for developing political skills. In that many of these new post–Vatican II programs emphasize, more so than in the past, church social teaching, greater opportunities exist for Catholics to learn how their religious values may intercept their political values.

Parish-affiliated Catholics show signs of greater agreement with the political positions of their bishops. Not only are they more likely than the general Catholic population to be Democrats (as are their bishops), they are also somewhat more likely to support the issue positions of their bishops on the death penalty, busing to achieve racial integration, and a nuclear weapons freeze. But even among practicing Catholics, there exist gaps between the political views of bishops and those of the laity. Even Catholics who attend church frequently are more conservative than their bishops on issues of crime (i.e., the death penalty) and more liberal (though less so than nonpracticing Catholics) on issues related to sexual freedom and abortion. While parish-connected Catholics are somewhat more likely to support busing, when it comes to homosexual rights, they are more conservative than their bishops and nonpracticing Catholics. While vocal advocates of civil rights for blacks, America's bishops have not pushed as aggressively for the civil rights of homosexuals, though a majority believe that homosexuals ought to be allowed to teach in the schools. Perhaps responding to official church teaching against homosexual practice, frequent church attenders are less sympathetic to this group. Infrequent church attenders are actually closer to their bishops on the question of whether homosexuals should be allowed to teach in the schools.

It is somewhat ironic, though not surprising, that as American bishops seek to influence the political values of their followers, American Catholics have become more independent-minded. Encouraged by the Council's call for greater lay participation in the Church and statements on the limits of clerical guidance, American Catholics are more discriminating in their willingness to accept pronouncements of the church hierarchy. When church leaders return to the authoritarian tactics of the past, many Catholics are turned off.

The fact that Catholics do not "obey" their bishops misses the point. The rules of the game have changed. Like a maturing young adult who becomes more independent, American Catholics have come of age. The Second Vatican Council marked a formal recognition of the maturity of lay Catholics and sought to foster a more adult relationship between the hierarchy and laity. This means, however, that a two-way dialogue is necessary.

The same dynamic that gives life to political democracy and freedom is at work within Catholicism. The basis of democratic government rests upon the principles of individual autonomy and personal responsibility. The evolution of democracy proceeds where access to education and open inquiry are secured. While the Roman Catholic Church is not predicated on a principle of democracy, it was forced to accept the realities of such political systems throughout the world. Through Vatican II it also endorsed the virtues of pluralism and individual freedom.

Like parents who must adjust to the maturation of their children entering adulthood, the church must change its relationship to its people in a rapidly modernizing and more sophisticated world. The discipline of the Church of the Middle Ages offered a security and stability needed to get Europe through potentially chaotic times. Widespread illiteracy rendered democratic government untenable. But with social, scientific, and economic advances, political and religious change would follow. At first reluctant to accept that change, the Church sought to tighten its grip. The Second Vatican Council, however, signified a formal reversal. The Church recognized the maturity of its people and loosened its reins. Mature adults are not receptive to orders; they must be shown the logic and reason for religious teaching. In recognition of this fact, Pope John XXIII maintained that the Church "considers that she meets the needs of the present day by demonstrating the validity of her teaching rather than by condemnations."[4]

Attempts to go back to pre–Vatican II ways will ultimately fail. Freedom once gained is not easily relinquished. The spirit of Vatican II cannot be constrained. Especially for American Catholics, that spirit is reinforced by a 200-year-old culture of pluralism and freedom. The Church and United States Catholic bishops can continue to be effective players in American politics, influencing cultural values, but only if they accept this reality.

NOTES

1. See David D. Laitin, "Religion, Political Culture, and the Weberian Tradition, *World Politics* (July 1978), p. 572.

2. Ibid.

3. Quoted in Loris F. Capovilla, "Reflections on the Twentieth Anniversary," in Alberic Stacpoole, ed., *Vatican II Revisited by Those who Were There* (Minneapolis: Winston Press, 1986), pp. 122–123.

4. Ibid.

References

Aliosi, Michael F. "Vatican II, Ecumenism and a Parsonian Analysis of Change," *Sociological Analysis* 49, no. 1 (Spring 1988), pp. 17–28.

Almond, Gabriel A. "Comparative Political Systems." *Journal of Politics* 18, no. 3 (August 1956), pp. 391–409.

Almond, Gabriel A., and G. Bingham Powell, Jr. *Comparative Politics: A Developmental Approach.* Boston: Little, Brown, 1966.

Almond, Gabriel A., and Sidney Verba. *The Civic Culture.* Princeton: Princeton University Press, 1963.

Beatty, Kathleen Murphy, and Oliver Walter. "Fundamentalists, Evangelicals and Politics." *American Politics Quarterly* 16, no. 1 (January 1988), pp. 43–59.

_____. "A Group Theory of Religion and Politics: The Clergy as Group Leaders." *Western Political Quarterly* 42, no. 1 (March 1989), pp. 129–146.

_____. "Religious Preference and Practice: Reevaluating Their Impact on Political Tolerance." *Public Opinion Quarterly* 48, no. 1B (Spring 1984), pp. 318–329.

Bell, Daniel. "The Return of the Sacred? The Argument on the Future of Religion." *British Journal of Sociology* 28, no. 4 (December 1977), pp. 419–449.

Bellah, Robert N., Richard Madsen, William M. Sullivan, Ann Swidler, and Steven M. Tipton. *Habits of the Heart.* New York: Harper and Row, 1985.

Benson, Peter L., and Dorothy L. Williams. *Religion on Capitol Hill: Myths and Realities.* New York: Oxford University Press, 1986.

Berelson, Bernard, Paul F. Lazarsfeld, and William N. McPhee. *Voting: A Study of Opinion Formation in a Presidential Campaign*. Chicago: University of Chicago Press, 1954.

Berelson, Bernard, and Gary A. Steiner. *Human Behavior: An Inventory of Scientific Findings*. New York: Harcourt, Brace and World, 1964.

Berger, Peter L. *The Sacred Canopy: Elements of a Sociological Theory of Religion*. Garden City, N.Y.: Doubleday, 1967.

Bianchi, Eugene C. "John XXIII, Vatican II, and American Catholicism." *Annals of the American Academy of Political and Social Science* 387 (January 1970), pp. 30–40.

Bill, James A., and Robert L. Hardgrave, Jr. *Comparative Politics: The Quest for Theory*. Lanham, Md.: University Press of America, 1981.

Bledstein, Burton J. *The Culture of Professionalism: the Middle Class and the Development of Higher Education in America*. New York: Norton, 1976.

Blickle, Peter. *Religion, Politics and Social Protest*. Boston: Allen and Unwin, 1984.

Boorstin, Daniel. *The Genius of American Politics*. Chicago: University of Chicago Press, 1953.

Brady, Henry E., and Paul M. Sniderman. "Attitude Attribution: A Group Basis for Political Reasoning." *American Political Science Review* 79, no. 4 (December 1985), pp. 1061–1078.

Broder, David S. *The Party's Over*. New York: Harper and Row, 1972.

Broughton, Walter. "Religiosity and Opposition to Church Social Action: A Test for a Weberian Hypothesis." *Review of Religious Research* 19, no. 2 (Winter 1978), pp. 154–166.

Brown, Robert McAfee. *Observer in Rome: A Protestant Report on the Vatican Council*. Garden City, N.Y.: Doubleday, 1964.

Butts, R. Freeman. *The American Tradition in Religion and Education*. Boston: Beacon Press, 1950.

Byrnes, Timothy A. *Catholic Bishops in American Politics*. Princeton: Princeton University Press, 1991.

Callahan, Daniel. *The Mind of the Catholic Layman*. New York: Scribner's, 1963.

Capovilla, Loris F. "Reflections on the Twentieth Anniversary." In Alberic Stacpoole, ed., *Vatican II Revisited by Those who Were There*. London: Geoffrey Chapman, 1986.

Carlen, Claudia. *The Papal Encyclicals*, vols. 1–5, 1740–1981. Wilmington, N.C.: McGrath, 1981.

Carrier, Herve. "Understanding Culture: The Ultimate Challenge of the World-Church?" In Joseph Gremillion, ed., *The Church and Culture since Vatican II: The Experience of North and Latin America*. Notre Dame, Ind.: University of Notre Dame Press, 1985.

Castelli, Jim. "A Tale of Two Cultures." *Notre Dame Magazine* 15 (Summer 1987), pp. 33–34.

Castelli, Jim, and Joseph Gremillion. *The Emerging Parish: The Notre Dame Study of Catholic Life since Vatican II*. San Francisco: Harper and Row, 1987.

Chardin, Teilhard de. *The Phenomenon of Man*. New York: Harper, 1959.

Charles, Rodger, and Drostan Maclaren. *The Social Teaching of Vatican II: Its Origin and Development*. San Francisco: Ignatius Press, 1982.

"The Church and Capitalism: A Report by Catholic Bishops on the U.S. Economy Will Cause a Furor." *Business Week*, November 12, 1984, pp. 104–112.

Commager, Henry Steele. *The American Mind: An Interpretation of American Thought and Character since the 1880s*. New Haven: Yale University Press, 1950.

Congar, Yves. "Moving Towards a Pilgrim Church." In Alberic Stacpoole, ed., *Vatican II Revisited by Those who Were There*. Minneapolis: Winston Press, 1986.

Conover, Pamela Johnston. "The Influence of Group Identification on Political Perception and Evaluation." *Journal of Politics* 46, no. 3 (August 1984), pp. 760–785.

Converse, Philip E. "The Nature of Belief Systems in Mass Publics." In David E. Apter, ed., *Ideology and Discontent*. New York: Free Press, 1964.

_____." Religion and Politics: The 1960 Election." In Angus Campbell, Philip E. Converse, Warren E. Miller, and Donald E. Stokes, eds., *Elections and the Political Order*. New York: Wiley, 1966.

_____. "Some Priority Variables in Comparative Electoral Research." In Richard Rose, ed., *Electoral Behavior: A Comparative Handbook*. New York: Free Press, 1974.

Cooney, Jim. *The American Pope*. New York: Times Books, 1984.

Corbett, Michael. *American Public Opinion: Trends, Processes, and Patterns*. New York: Longman, 1991.

Cotton, John. *An Exposition upon the Thirteenth Chapter of the Revelation*. 1655. Reprinted in part in Edmund S. Morgan, *Puritan Political Ideas*. Indianapolis: Bobbs-Merrill, 1965.

Crosby, David F. *God, Church, and Flag: Senator Joseph R. McCarthy and the Catholic Church, 1950–1957*. Chapel Hill: University of North Carolina Press, 1978.

Cross, Robert D. *The Emergence of Liberal Catholicism in America*. Cambridge, Mass.: Harvard University Press, 1958.

Crotty, William, and Gary Jacobson. *American Parties in Decline*. 2nd ed. Boston: Little, Brown, 1984.

Dahrendorf, Ralf. *Class and Class Conflict in Industrial Society*. Stanford: Stanford University Press, 1959.

Daniel-Rops, Henri. *The Second Vatican Council: the Story Behind the Ecumenical Council of Pope John XXIII*. New York: Hawthorn Books, 1962.

Davidson, James D., Ronald Elly, Thomas Hull, and Donald Nead. "Increasing Church Involvement in Social Concerns: A Model for Human Ministries." *Review of Religious Research* 20, no. 3 (Summer 1979), pp. 291–314.

Dexter, Henry Martyn. *The Congregationalism of the Last Three Hundred Years As Seen in Its Literature: With Special Reference to Certain Recondite, Neglected, or Disputed Passages.* New York: Harper and Brothers, Publishers, 1880.

Diamant, Alfred. "The Nature of Political Development." In Jason L. Finkle and Richard W. Gable, eds., *Political Development and Social Change.* New York: Wiley, 1966.

Dinges, William D. "Ritual Conflict as Social Conflict: Liturgical Reform in the Roman Catholic Church." *Sociological Analysis* 48, no. 2 (Summer 1987), pp. 138–157.

Dionne, E. J., Jr. "Catholics and the Democrats: Estrangement but Not Desertion." In Seymour M. Lipset, ed., *Party Coalitions in the 1980s.* San Francisco: Institute for Contemporary Studies, 1981.

Dixon, Robert, and Dean Hoge. "Models and Priorities of the Catholic Church as Held by Suburban Laity." *Review of Religious Research* 20, no. 2 (Spring 1979), pp. 150–167.

Dohen, Dorothy. *Nationalism and American Catholicism.* New York: Oxford University Press, 1968.

Dolan, Jay P. *The American Catholic Experience: A History from Colonial Times to the Present.* Garden City, N.Y.: Doubleday, 1985.

Donegani, Jean-Marie. "The Political Cultures of French Catholicism." In Suzanne Berger, ed., *Religion in West European Politics.* London: Frank Cass, 1982.

D'Souza, Dinesh. "The Bishops as Pawns: Behind the Scenes at the U.S. Catholic Conference." *Policy Review* (Fall 1985), pp. 50–56.

Duff, Edward. "The Church and American Public Life." In Philip Gleason, ed., *Contemporary Catholicism in the United States.* Notre Dame, Ind.: University of Notre Dame Press, 1969.

Dulong, Renaud. "Christian Militants in the French Left." In Suzanne Berger, ed., *Religion in West European Politics.* London: Frank Cass, 1982.

Dunn, Charles W., ed. *Religion in American Politics.* Washington, D.C.: Congressional Quarterly, 1989.

Dulles, Avery. "The Teaching Auhority of the Bishops' Conference." *America,* June 11, 1983, pp. 453–455.

Durkheim, Emile. *The Elementary Forms of the Religious Life.* Trans. Joseph Ward Swain. New York: Free Press, 1965.

Dwyer, Judith A., ed. *The Catholic Bishops and Nuclear War: A Critique and Analysis of the Pastoral "The Challenge of Peace."* Washington, D.C.: Georgetown University Press, 1984.

Eisenhofer, Ludwig. *The Liturgy of the Roman Rite.* New York: Herder and Herder, 1953.

Ellis, John Tracy. *American Catholicism*, 2nd ed. Chicago: University of Chicago Press, 1969.

_____. *American Catholics and the Intellectual Life*. Chicago: Heritage Foundation, 1956.

_____. "Religious Freedom: An American Reaction." In Alberic Stacpoole, ed., *Vatican II Revisited by Those who Were There*. Minneapolis: Winston Press, 1986.

Evans, Bernard. "Campaign for Human Development: Church Involvement in Social Change." *Review of Religious Research* 20, no. 3 (Summer 1979), pp. 264–278.

Fee, Joan L. "Political Continuity and Change." In Andrew M. Greeley, William C. McCready, and Kathleen McCourt, *Catholic Schools in a Declining Church*. Kansas City: Sheed and Ward, 1976.

Fenton, John H. *The Catholic Vote*. New Orleans: Hauser Press, 1960.

Feuerherd, Joe. "Death Penalty Makes Political Hay: Bishop Puts Lawmaker on New York Hot Seat." *National Catholic Reporter* 26, no. 32 (June 1, 1990), p. 3.

Flannery, Austin P., ed. *Documents of Vatican II*. Grand Rapids, Mich.: Eerdmans, 1975.

Fogarty, Gerald P., ed. *Patterns of Episcopal Leadership*. New York: Macmillan, 1989.

Formicola, Jo Renee. "American Catholic Political Theology." In Mary C. Segers, ed., *Church Polity and American Politics: Issues in Contemporary American Catholicism*. New York: Garland, 1990.

Fremantle, Anne. *The Papal Encyclicals in Their Historical Context*. New York: Mentor-Omega Books, 1963.

Friedrich, Carl J. *Transcendent Justice: The Religious Foundations of Constitutionalism*. Durham, N.C.: Duke University Press, 1964.

Fuller, Edmund. *God in the White House: The Faiths of American Presidents*. New York: Crown, 1968.

Gallup, George, Jr., and Jim Castelli. *The American Catholic People: Their Beliefs, Practices, and Values. Garden City, N.Y.: Doubleday, 1987.*

Geertz, Clifford. "Religion as a Cultural System." In Donald R. Cutler, ed., *The Religious Situation*. Boston: Beacon Press, 1968.

Gelm, Richard J. "Religion and Partisan Preference in Europe." Paper presented at the 1989 Annual Meeting of the American Political Science Association, Atlanta, Georgia.

Gilhooley, Leonard. *Contradiction and Dilemma: Orestes Brownson and the American Idea*. New York: Fordham University Press, 1972.

Gorski, Mary. "Weakland Urges Abortion Shifts." *National Catholic Reporter* 26, no. 32 (June 1, 1990), p. 1.

Gould, William J., Jr. "The Challenge of Liberal Political Culture in the Thought of John Courtney Murray." Paper presented at the 1990 Annual Meeting of the American Political Science Association, San Francisco, California.

Greeley, Andrew M. *The American Catholic: A Social Portrait.* New York: Basic Books, 1977.

_____. *American Catholics since the Council: An Unauthorized Report.* Chicago: Thomas More Press, 1985.

_____. *The Catholic Priest in the United States: Sociological Investigations.* Washington, D.C.: United States Catholic Conference, 1972.

_____. "Council or Encyclical." *Review of Religious Research* 18 no. 1 (Fall 1976), pp. 3–24.

_____. "How Conservative Are American Catholics?" *Political Science Quarterly* 92, no. 2 (Summer 1977), pp. 199–218.

Greeley, Andrew M., and Michael Hout. "The Center Doesn't Hold: Church Attendance in the United States, 1940–1984." *American Sociological Review* 52, no. 3 (June 1987), pp. 325–345.

Greer, Scott. "Catholic Voters and the Democratic Party." *Public Opinion Quarterly* 25, no. 4 (Winter 1961), pp. 611–625.

Groth, Alexander J. *Progress and Chaos: Modernization and Rediscovery of Religion and Authority.* Malabar, Fla.: Robert E. Kreiger, 1984.

Grupp, Frederick W., and William M. Newman. "Political Ideology and Religious Preference: The John Birch Society and the Americans for Democratic Action." *Journal for the Scientific Study of Religion* 12, no. 4 (December 1973), pp. 401–413.

Guitton, Jean. *The Church and the Laity: From Newman to Vatican II.* Staten Island, N.Y.: Alba House, 1965.

Guth, James L. "Pastoral Politics in the 1988 Election: Protestant Clergy and Political Mobilization." Paper presented at the 1989 Annual Meeting of the American Political Science Association, Atlanta, Georgia.

Guth, James L., Ted G. Jelen, Lyman A. Kellstedt, Corwin E. Smidt, and Kenneth D. Wald. "The Politics of Religion in America: Issues for Investigation." *American Politics Quarterly* 16, no. 3 (July 1988), pp. 357–397.

Hadden, Jeffrey K. *The Gathering Storm in the Churches.* Garden City, N.Y.: Doubleday, 1969.

Halpern, Manfred. "Toward Further Modernization of the Study of New Nations." *World Politics* 17. (October 1964), pp. 157–181.

Hanline, C. Jeanne, ed. *Official Catholic Directory.* Wilmette, Ill.: Kenedy and Sons, 1988.

Hanna, Mary T. *Catholics and American Politics.* Cambridge, Mass.: Harvard University Press, 1979.

_____. "Bishops as Political Leaders." In Charles W. Dunn, ed., *Religion in American Politics.* Washington, D.C.: CQ Press, 1989.

Harding, Stephen, and David Phillips with Michael Fogarty. *Contrasting Values in Western Europe.* London: Macmillan, 1986.

Hartz, Louis. *The Liberal Tradition in America.* New York: Harcourt, Brace, 1955.

Hegel, G.F.W. *The Philosophy of History.* Trans. J. Sibree. New York: Willey Book Co., 1956.

_____. *The Philosophy of Right*. Trans. T. M. Knox. London: Oxford University Press, 1967.

Heimert, Alan. *Religion and the American Mind*. Cambridge, Mass.: Harvard University Press, 1966.

Hennesey, James. "Roman Catholics and American Politics, 1900–1960: Altered Circumstances, Continuing Patterns." In Mark A. Noll, ed., *Religion and American Politics: From the Colonial Period to the 1980s*. New York: Oxford University Press, 1990.

Hitchcock, James. *The Decline and Fall of Radical Catholicism*. New York: Herder and Herder, 1971.

Hobbes, Thomas. *The Leviathan*. Cambridge, England: Cambridge University Press, 1990.

Hoge, Dean, and Robert Dixon. *Research on Men's Vocations to the Priesthood and Religious Life*. Washington, D.C.: United States Catholic Conference Office of Research, 1984.

Huntington, Samuel P. *American Politics: The Promise of Disharmony*. Cambridge, Mass.: Belknap Press, 1981.

_____. *Political Order in Changing Societies*. New Haven: Yale University Press, 1968.

John XXIII. *Mater et magistra*, 1961.

_____. *Pacem in terris*, 1963.

John Paul II. *Centesimuss annus*, 1991.

_____. *Laborem exercens*, 1981.

_____. *Sollicitudo rei socialis*, 1987.

Johnson, Chalmers. *Revolutionary Change*. Boston: Little, Brown, 1966.

Johnson, Stephen D., and Joseph B. Tamney, eds. *The Political Role of Religion in the United States*. Boulder, Colo.: Westview Press, 1986.

Johnstone, Robert L. "Public Images of Protestant Ministers and Catholic Priests: An Empirical Study of Anti-Clericalism in the U.S." *Sociological Analysis* 33, no. 1 (Spring 1972), pp. 34–49.

Jorstad, Erling. *The Politics of Moralism: The New Christian Right in American Life*. Minneapolis: Augsburg, 1981.

Kelly, George Anthony. *The Crisis of Authority*. Chicago: Regnery Gateway, 1982.

Kelly, George Armstrong. *Politics and Religious Consciousness in America*. New Brunswick: Transaction Books, 1984.

Kennedy, Eugene C., and Victor J. Heckler. *The Catholic Priest in the United States: Psychological Investigations*. Washington, D.C.: United States Catholic Conference, 1972.

KRC Research and Consulting, Inc. "Summary of Findings: National Poll on the Catholic Church and Abortion." Prepared for Catholics for a Free Choice. #2640, October 1990.

Kselman, Thomas. *Miracles and Prophecies in Nineteenth-Century France*. New Brunswick: Rutgers University Press, 1983.

Laitin, David D. "Religion, Political Culture, and the Weberian Tradition." *World Politics* 30 (July 1978), pp. 563–592.

Laumann, Edward O., and David R. Segal. "Status Inconsistency and Ethnoreligious Group Membership as Determinants of Social Participation and Political Attitudes." *American Journal of Sociology* 77, no. 1 (July 1971), pp. 36–61.

Lawler, Philip. *How Bishops Decide*. Washington, D.C.: Ethics and Public Policy Center, 1986.

Lazarsfeld, Paul F., Bernard Berelson, and Hazel Gaudet. *The People's Choice: How the Voter Makes up His Mind in a Presidential Campaign*. New York: Columbia University Press, 1948.

LeBlanc, Hugh L., and Mary Beth Merrin. "Mass Belief Systems Revisited." *Journal of Politics* 39, no. 4 (November 1977), pp. 1082–1087.

Leege, David C. "Catholics and the Civic Order: Parish Participation, Politics, and Civic Participation." *The Review of Politics* 50, no. 4 (Fall 1988), pp. 704–736.

Leege, David C., and Thomas A. Trozzolo. "Religious Values and Parish Participation: The Paradox of Individual Needs in a Communitarian Church." Notre Dame Study of Catholic Parish Life, no. 4, June 1985.

Lenski, Gerhard. *The Religious Factor: A Sociological Study of Religion's Impact on Politics, Economics, and Family Life*. Garden City, N.Y.: Doubleday–Anchor, 1963.

Leo XIII. *Rerum novarum*, 1891.

Lerner, Robert, Stanley Rothman, and S. Robert Lichter. "Christian Religious Elites." *Public Opinion* (March/April 1989), pp. 54–59.

Lernoux, Penny. *People of God: The Struggle for World Catholicism*. New York: Viking, 1989.

Levine, Daniel H. "Religion and Politics in Comparative and Historical Perspective." *Comparative Politics* 19, no. 1 (October 1986), pp. 95–122.

Lijphart, Arend. *The Politics of Accommodation: Pluralism and Democracy in the Netherlands*. Berkeley: University of California Press, 1968.

Lipset, Seymour Martin. "Three Decades of the Radical Right: Coughlinites, McCarthyites, and Birchers." In Daniel Bell, ed., *The Radical Right*. Garden City, N.Y.: Doubleday-Anchor, 1964.

Luckmann, Thomas. *The Invisible Religion. New York: Macmillan, 1967*.

Machiavelli, Niccolò. *Discourses*. In Max Lerner, ed., *The Prince and the Discourses*. New York: Modern Library, 1950.

Maddox, William S. "Changing Electoral Coalitions from 1952–1976." *Social Science Quarterly* 60, no. 2 (September 1979), pp. 309–313.

Martin, David. "Religion and Public Values: A Catholic-Protestant Contrast." *Review of Religious Research* 26, no. 4 (June 1985), pp. 313–331.

Marty, Martin. *Religion and Republic: The American Circumstance*. Boston: Beacon Press, 1987.

Mayhew, Jonathan. *A Discourse Concerning Unlimited Submission and Non-Resistance to the Higher Powers: With Some Reflections on the Resis-*

tance Made to King Charles I. 1750. Reprinted in part in Edmund S. Morgan, *Puritan Political Ideas.* Indianapolis: Bobbs-Merrill, 1965.

McAvoy, Thomas T. *The Great Crisis in American Catholic History 1895–1900.* Chicago: H. Regnery, 1957.

McBrien, Richard P. *Catholicism.* Minneapolis: Winston Press, 1980.

————. "A Papal Attack on Vatican II." *New York Times,* March 12, 1990, p. A15.

McClory, Robert. "Catholic Bishop's Ultra-Orthodoxy May Not Play in Peoria." *National Catholic Reporter* 27, no. 30 (May 24, 1991), p. 6.

McClosky, Herbert, and John Zaller. *The American Ethos: Public Attitudes toward Capitalism and Democracy.* Cambridge, Mass.: Harvard University Press, 1984.

McKeown, Elizabeth. "The National Bishops' Conference: An Analysis of Its Origins." *Catholic Historical Review* 66 (October 1980), pp. 565–576.

McMillan, Margaret. *The Life of Rachel McMillan.* London: J. M. Dent, 1927.

McNeill, John T., ed. *Calvin: On God and Political Duty.* Indianapolis: Bobbs-Merrill, 1956.

Michelat, Guy, and Michel Simon. "Religion, Class, and Politics." *Comparative Politics* 10, no. 1 (October 1977).

Milhaven, Anne Lally. "Dissent Within the U.S. Church: An Interview with Charles Curran." In Mary C. Segers, ed., *Church Polity and American Politics: Issues in Contemporary American Catholicism.* New York: Garland, 1990.

Miller, Abraham. "Ethnicity and Party Identification: Continuation of a Theoretical Dialogue." *Western Political Quarterly* 27, no. 3 (September 1974), pp. 479–490.

Miller, Perry. *Errand into the Wilderness.* Cambridge, Mass.: Harvard University Press, 1956.

Miller, William Lee. "American Religion and American Political Attitudes." In James Ward Smith and A. Leland Jamison, eds., *Religious Perspectives in American Culture.* Princeton: Princeton University Press, 1961.

Montesquieu, Charles-Louis de Secondat. *The Spirit of the Laws.* Trans. Thomas Nugent. New York: Hafner, 1949.

Morgan, Edmund S. *Puritan Political Ideas.* Indianapolis: Bobbs-Merrill, 1965.

Murray, John Courtney. *We Hold These Truths.* New York: Sheed and Ward, 1960.

Musetto, Andrew P. "Innovators in the Catholic Church." *Review of Religious Research* 17, no. 1 (Fall 1975), pp. 28–36.

National Conference of Catholic Bishops. "The Challenge of Peace: God's Promise and Our Response." Washington, D.C.: United States Catholic Conference, 1983.

————. "Economic Justice for All: Catholic Social Teaching and the U.S. Economy." Washington, D.C.: United States Catholic Conference, 1986.

Neuhaus, Richard John. *The Catholic Moment*. San Francisco: Harper and Row, 1987.

Nie, Norman, and Kristi Anderson. "Mass Belief Systems Revisited: Political Change and Attitude Structure." *Journal of Politics* 36, no. 3 (August 1974), pp. 540–591.

Nisbet, Robert A. *Social Change and History*. New York: Oxford University Press, 1969.

Nolan, Hugh J., ed. *Pastoral Letters of the United States Catholic Bishops*. Vols. 1–4, 1792–1983. Washington, D.C.: United States Catholic Conference, 1984.

———, ed. *Pastoral Letters of the United States Catholic Bishops*. Vol. 5, 1983–1988. Washington, D.C.: United States Catholic Conference, 1989.

Norpoth, Helmut, and Jerrold G. Rusk. "Partisan Dealignment in the American Electorate: Itemizing the Deductions since 1964." *American Political Science Review* 76 (September 1982), pp. 522–537.

Novak, Michael. *The Open Church*. New York: Macmillan, 1964.

———. *The Spirit of Democratic Capitalism*. New York: Simon and Schuster, 1982.

O'Brien, David. *Public Catholicism*. New York: Macmillan, 1989.

Ochs, Stephen. *Desegregating the Altar: The Josephites and the Struggle for Black Priests, 1871–1960*. Baton Rouge: Louisiana State University Press, 1990.

O'Dea, Thomas F. *American Catholic Dilemma*. New York: Sheed and Ward, 1958.

———. *The Catholic Crisis*. Boston: Beacon Press, 1968.

O'Hara, Thomas J. "The Catholic Lobby in Washington: Pluralism and Diversity among U.S. Catholics." In Mary C. Segers, ed., *Church Polity and American Politics: Issues in Contemporary American Catholicism*. New York: Garland, 1990.

Ornstein, Norman J., Thomas E. Mann, and Michael J. Malbin. *Vital Statistics on Congress: 1991–1992*. Washington, D.C.: Congressional Quarterly, 1992.

Ozment, Steven. *Protestants: The Birth of a Revolution*. New York: Doubleday, 1992.

Parenti, Michael. "Political Values and Religious Culture: Jews, Catholics and Protestants." *Journal for the Scientific Study of Religion* 6, no. 1 (Spring 1967), pp. 259–269.

Parsons, Talcott. *The Social System*. New York: Free Press, 1964.

Paul VI. Octogesima adveniens, 1971.

———. *Populorum progressio*, 1967.

Penning, James M. "The Political Behavior of American Catholics: An Assessment of the Impact of Group Integration vs. Group Identification." *Western Political Quarterly* 41, no. 2 (June 1988), pp. 289–308.

Percheron, Annick. "Religious Acculturation and Political Socialisation in France." In Suzanne Berger, ed., *Religion in West European Politics*. London: Frank Cass,1983.

Phillips, Kevin. *The Emerging Republican Majority*. New York: Doubleday-Anchor, 1969.

Pius X. *Pascendi dominici gregis*, 1907.

Pius XI. *Quadragesimo anno*, 1931.

Poggi, Gianfranco. *Catholic Action in Italy*. Stanford: Stanford University Press, 1967.

Pye, Lucian W. *Aspects of Political Development*. Boston: Little, Brown, 1966.

_____. "Political Culture." *International Encyclopedia of the Social Sciences*. New York: Macmillian and Free Press, 1968, pp. 218–225.

Quinley, Harold E. *The Prophetic Clergy: Social Activism among Protestant Ministers*. New York: Wiley, 1974.

Reese, Thomas J. *Archbishop: Inside the Power Structure of the American Catholic Church*. New York: Harper and Row, 1989.

_____. "A Survey of the American Bishops." *America,* November 12, 1983, pp. 285–288.

Reichley, James A. *Religion in American Public Life*. Washington, D.C.: The Brookings Institution, 1985.

Renna, Thomas. *Church and State in Medieval Europe 1050–1314*. Dubuque: Kendall/Hunt, 1974.

Riggs, Fred W. *Administration in Developing Countries: The Theory of Prismatic Society*. Boston: Houghton Mifflin, 1964.

Roof, Wade Clark. "Concepts and Indicators of Religious Commitment: A Critical Review." In Robert Wuthnow, ed., *The Religious Dimension: New Directions in Quantitative Research*. New York: Academic Press, 1979.

Rose, Richard, and D. Urwin. "Social Cohesion, Political Parties and Strains in Regimes." *Comparative Political Studies* 2, no. 1 (April 1969), pp. 7–67.

Rosenthal, Alan. "On Analyzing States." In Alan Rosenthal and Maureen Moakley, eds., *The Political Life of the American States*. New York: Praeger, 1984.

Rousseau, Jean-Jacques. *The Social Contract*. Trans. Maurice Cranston. New York: Penguin Books, 1968.

Royal, Robert, ed. *Challenge and Response: Critiques of the Catholic Bishops' Draft Letter on the U.S. Economy*, vol. 57. Washington, D.C.: Ethics and Public Policy Center, 1985.

Schlesinger, Arthur M., Jr. *Orestes A. Brownson: A Pilgrim's Progress*. New York: Octagon Books, 1963.

Schuyler, Joseph B. *Northern Parish*. Chicago: Loyola University Press, 1960.

Seidman, Aaron. "Church and State in the Early Years of the Massachusetts Bay Colony." *New England Quarterly* 18 (March–December 1945), pp. 211–233.

Shelley, Thomas J. "Paul J. Hallinan." In Gerald P. Fogarty, ed., *Patterns of Episcopal Leadership*. New York: Macmillan, 1989, pp. 235–249.

Smith, Donald. *Religion and Political Development*. Boston: Little, Brown, 1970.

Smith, Martin. "Retrogressive Bishops." *Sacramento Bee*, November 20, 1989, p. B4.

Spotts, Frederic. *The Churches and Politics in Germany*. Middletown, Conn.: Wesleyan University Press, 1973.

Stacpoole, Alberic, ed. *Vatican II Revisited by Those who Were There*. London: Geoffrey Chapman, 1986.

Steinfels, Peter. "Bishop Lends Ear to Ideas on Abortion." *New York Times*, March 27, 1990, p. A9.

Stout, Harry S. "Rhetoric and Reality in the Early Republic: The Case of the Federalist Clergy." In Mark A. Noll, ed., *Religion and American Politics: From the Colonial Period to the 1980s*. New York: Oxford University Press, 1990.

Tamney, Joseph B., Ronald Burton, and Stephen Johnson. "Christianity, Social Class, and the Catholic Bishops' Economic Policy." *Sociological Analysis* 49 (December 1988), pp. 78–96.

Thung, Mady A., Gert J. Peelen, and Marten C. Kingmans. "Dutch Pillarisation on the Move? Political Destabilisation and Religious Change." In Suzanne Berger, ed., *Religion in West European Politics*. London: Frank Cass, 1982.

Tillich, Paul. *Theology of Culture*. Oxford, England: Oxford University Press, 1964.

Toolin, Cynthia. "American Civil Religion from 1789–1981." *Review of Religious Research* 25, no. 1 (September 1983), pp. 39–48.

Treacy, Gerald. *Five Great Encyclicals*. New York: Paulist Press, 1939.

United States Catholic Bishops. "Partners in the Mystery of Redemption: A Pastoral Response to Women's Concerns for Church and Society." First draft, in *Origins* 17, no. 45 (April 21, 1988), pp. 757–788.

Verba, Sidney. "Comparative Political Culture." In Lucian Pye and Sidney Verba, eds., *Political Culture and Political Development*. Princeton: Princeton University Press, 1965.

Von Hildebrand, Dietrich. *The Devastated Vineyard*. Chicago: Franciscan Herald Press, 1973.

Wakin, Edward, and Joseph F. Scheuer. *The De-Romanization of the American Catholic Church*. New York: Macmillan, 1966.

Wald, Kenneth D. *Religion and Politics in the United States*. New York: St. Martin's Press, 1987.

Wald, Kenneth D., Dennis E. Owen, and Samuel S. Hill, Jr. "Churches and Political Communities." *American Political Science Review* 82, no. 2 (June 1988), pp. 531–548.

Wattenberg, Martin P. *The Decline of American Political Parties, 1952–1984*. Cambridge, Mass.: Harvard University Press, 1986.

Weber, Max. *The Protestant Ethic and the Spirit of Capitalism*. Trans. Talcott Parsons. New York: Scribner's, 1958.

Welch, Michael, David C. Leege, Kenneth D. Wald, and Lyman A Kellstedt. "Pastoral Cues and Congregational Responses: Evidence from the 1989 NES Pilot Study." Paper presented at the 1990 Annual Meeting of the American Political Science Association, San Francisco, California.

Wertman, Douglas A. "The Catholic Church and Italian Politics: The Impact of Secularisation." In Suzanne Berger, ed., *Religion in West European Politics*. London: Frank Cass, 1982.

Whitehead, James D., and Evelyn Eaton Whitehead. *The Emerging Laity: Returning Leadership to the Community of Faith*. Garden City, N.Y.: Doubleday, 1986.

Whyte, John H. *Catholics in Western Democracies: A Study in Political Behavior*. Dublin, Ireland: Gill and Macmillan, 1981.

Wills, Garry. *Under God: Religion and American Politics*. New York: Simon and Schuster, 1990.

Wilson, Bryan. *Religion in Sociological Perspective*. Oxford, England: Oxford University Press, 1982.

Windsor, Pat. "Cincinnati Prelate with a 'German Soul' Leads U.S. Bishops." *National Catholic Reporter* 26, no. 33 (June 15, 1990), p. 8.

Winters, Francis X. "Bishops and Scholars: The Peace Pastoral under Siege." *Review of Politics* 48, no. 1 (Winter 1986), pp. 31–59.

Wood, Gordon S. *The Creation of the American Republic*. Williamsburg, Va.: Institute of Early American History and Culture, 1969.

Yinger, J. Milton. *The Scientific Study of Religion*. London: Macmillan, 1970.

Yzermas, Vincent, ed. *American Participation in the Second Vatican Council*. New York: Sheed and Ward, 1967.

Index

About the Author

RICHARD J. GELM is Assistant Professor of Political Science at the University of La Verne.